Neanderthals

The Genesis and Evolution of the Human Race

(A Read-in-one-sitting Tale About Neanderthals in Ancient Rome)

Kaylee Wilson

Published By **Jackson Denver**

Kaylee Wilson

All Rights Reserved

Neanderthals: The Genesis and Evolution of the Human Race (A Read-in-one-sitting Tale About Neanderthals in Ancient Rome)

ISBN 978-1-77485-715-1

No part of this guidebook shall be reproduced in any form without permission in writing from the publisher except in the case of brief quotations embodied in critical articles or reviews.

Legal & Disclaimer

The information contained in this ebook is not designed to replace or take the place of any form of medicine or professional medical advice. The information in this ebook has been provided for educational & entertainment purposes only.

The information contained in this book has been compiled from sources deemed reliable, and it is accurate to the best of the Author's knowledge; however, the Author cannot guarantee its accuracy and validity and cannot be held liable for any errors or omissions. Changes are periodically made to this book. You must consult your doctor or get professional medical advice before using any of the suggested remedies, techniques, or information in this book.

Upon using the information contained in this book, you agree to hold harmless the Author from and against any damages, costs, and expenses, including any legal fees potentially resulting from the application of any of the information provided by this guide. This disclaimer applies to any damages or injury caused by the use and application, whether directly or indirectly, of any advice or information presented, whether for breach of contract, tort, negligence, personal injury, criminal intent, or under any other cause of action.

You agree to accept all risks of using the information presented inside this book. You need to consult a professional medical practitioner in order to ensure you are both able and healthy enough to participate in this program.

TABLE OF CONTENTS

Introduction 1

Chapter 1: Learning Agriculture 10

Chapter 2: Creation Of Language 16

Chapter 3: "Philophers And Sophists" 29

Chapter 4: Confucius In The Fifth Century Bc In China 45

Chapter 5: The First Hominin Australopithecus 63

Chapter 6: Our African Origins - Homo Habilis 98

Chapter 7: The Spear Thrower - Homo Heidelbergensis 146

Chapter 8: Our Emergence - Homo Sapiens 175

Introduction

Human beings are human. It is now the time that we need to start understanding ourselves, examining the state of the man generally, studying his history and culture and learning about the various social structures that shape the way he behaves and defines the relationships he has with other people.

Humankind has made huge strides in every field of research, and the human mind has been successful in unravelling some of the mysteries of the universe, and breaking some of its mysteries even as the human experience in many ways remain a mystery to him that we are able to understand almost nothing. There are entire cultures and societies which we know very little concerning, in spite of the increasing interest that has been gaining momentum in the study of human societies in various parts of the globe, particularly the study of tiny tribal communities that live in remote areas, and the need to understand their customs and traditions, as well as their past whenever possible.

This is the reason we will attempt, in a short amount to define the various stages of human intellectual growth throughout his .journey through his life

Man's appearance on Earth is an unidentified time period that has caused huge controversy among scientists. Man has been around since his arrival on the the earth over a number of periods of time, which we'll discuss in general:

Historical and Prehistory eras separated by the invention, discovery, or understanding of writing as early as 3500 BC. In terms of prehistoric times they are comprised from prehistoric times. They are part of Old Stone Age, which is the period in which people used stone-carved tools and the age grew until he was able to learn agriculture. In the Neolithic Age, it is the time when polished stones were utilized and until the discovery and understanding of the human race to write.

For the most important phases of the eras of the past, they are comprised of four periods:

The first period of the ancient era starts at the age of 3500 BC and concludes .with the end of the Roman Empire in 476 AD The second is the Medieval Age, which began in 476 .AD until the discovery of America in 1492 AD The third phase of the modern age, which began .from 1492 AD until the French Revolution in 1789 AD Then comes the fourth stage that is known as the modern era .which started in 1789 AD up to today.

Human thought's history is a vast archive that contains a vast record of both universal and human experiences. Human history is an overall structure in which the cognitive and psychological results of the experiences of humanity throughout the universe are contained .and even the experiences of living within the universe.

The human problems and his personality, psyche desires, and needs are unique, diverse as well as endless, resulting from the conditions that define his existence. Human beings are required to think, to create, and to explore. The person must change his perspective on the environment around him. or he altered his method of thinking, his scientific or literary theories, and the entire framework of his thoughts that changed the real world. This also changed his behavior, actions, and general actions when confronting the reality of our world and seeking to understand how to reflect and improve it. In the hope of conquering the challenges of nature by understanding them and adapting these obstacles to .his advantages

The human experiences through time are a fact that we can't deny as it remains in our collective memory as well as in the collective memory of all the world. Man has come up with concepts that have been the pivotal factors that influenced the changes in the nature of life and the way we live within it. They also affected them by introducing new ideas, customs .and rules

It was a result of the technological advancements which had led to the advancement of the arts, science and literature, which reflected this new and important advancement in various degrees on the world of reality lifestyles, the way of life and the broad vision of the world and attempting to alter it.

to benefit to benefit mankind. To control nature to achieve the highest levels of material wealth and happiness for the majority of people as well as for the benefit of mankind. This has been since humans started to exert control over nature. We will review several of the most significant of them in the following order

The first-ever developed

mental and psychological capabilities of the very first human being were the reason behind his distinctiveness and uniqueness. There are elements in nature that connect and transcend the physical realm these are the realms that can be described as"the .worlds of the mind and soul

Before we are able to understand the mental and emotional energies of a person in the first stages of thought it is essential to understand the brain's thinking processes of the human brain, since our mind acts as the moral code of the brain's physical structure which is why the mind is able to perform its task. In it, the personality of the individual that separates the person from other people is determined. The brain is thought to be the central command centre in which information is collected from the external world via the organs that are connected to the external environment. after which the different interactions occur within it to take the required .decisions

intelligence is the capability to solve problems in a rational procedure (may it be mathematical, logical or philosophical, or in any other field). Additionally, intelligence refers to the capacity to react correctly to events in .life as a whole and within society specifically.

Human memory is the capacity to represent information in a selective manner. The human memory as an information-processing system includes stages (the coding stage associated with education - the retention and storage stage, which is the focus of . (memory The recall or retrieval stage

Human thought as a whole is the result of these accumulations and experiences that different nations have experienced and the involvement and imagination of thought leaders in various time and places. Human beings have the capacity to communicate the issues of understanding and feeling was manifested, and with the idea of freedom and distinction was formulated too. The past was when humans considered the direction of the universe and what the universe was and what its place within the universe. The construction of civilizations has gone through several stages, various ideas have contributed to its growth and advancement, while other .ideas attempted to destroy and deform it.

Additionally, the way of thinking differs from one individual to the next, and in all, there are four kinds of thinking styles:

.Thinking of external influences 1.

2. Independent thinking that is based on an inner revelation.

3. The collective mind is focused on a single answer to specific problems.

4. An open mind, which is distinguished by the capacity to generate numerous new ideas.

So far, the human race has been trying to save the human civilization's foundation and ensure that it will not collapse and disappear like it did to civilizations that were destroyed and destroyed in the past throughout the history of humanity. We wish it succeed.

The scientific theories and ideas are in essence human inventions that lack identity, no nationality and have no connection to them, except for humanity. Humanity's thinkers stepped off from their confined world all over the globe and transcended all boundaries with their theories and ideas included the entire world.

They are a series of continuous intellectual loops that were on the pages of space and time, and their influence was seen in the pages of our time and history. This is an human inheritance which is inherited from the preceding without identification or any other considerations. It has been stripped of its unique character and placed in an epic in human intelligence time. Human intelligence and individual talent rule the world. They are the human intellectual struggle to conquer the challenges .and the challenges of nature

Chapter 1: Learning Agriculture

The Neolithic period was marked by polished stone machinery, and this time was defined by the advent of farming alongside hunting and the establishment of certain areas to collect crops from the agriculture. Man moved from hunting and picking to the practice of agriculture by .observation and experimentation

For over a decade humankind depended on nature to satisfy his needs for food. He was forced to satisfy his time with gathering and harvesting wild grains and fruits as well as grains, fruits and other items made by nature. And at a later time after many thousands in time, the existence of the primitive man was enriched and eventually reached stability farming, the practice of agriculture as well as the domestication and breeding of livestock in order to profit in their food, their milk, and wool. It is one of the elements of stability. Also, the abolition of continuous moving from one location to another, leading to the .emergence of cities and art

He was taught to plant seeds into the earth to increase the quantity of food available to satisfy the demands of his family and was the beginning of agriculture, which is thought to be one of the most significant achievements that man has made it through the years. He began to learn about the non-food plants and plant the seeds that were good. He utilized digging sticks, which was also used to harvest the crops, and he started to provide the food and other needs in addition. The man changed from being a food collector into an individual producer as his diet increased, and he was able to meet his requirements and had a variety of food. The rise of agriculture as well as livestock domestication brought about stability in the human race. This stability led to the construction of villages and using stronger material for construction. He also cooks his meals and weaves his pets.

Changes that increased the quality of agriculture

In reality, the mental capacity of man had reached an age of maturity that allowed him to take this leap. In addition, the long-standing mastery of nature and his capacity to observe and test. An experience that has been accumulated for a long time in the subconscious can at the time to emerge as an internal element that is correlated to a variety of external interactions like the physical environment, manual skills and so on. This change occurred during the Stone Age, with an intellectual revolution that extended beyond the agricultural revolution to other developments that improved the level of performance in farming and increased yield. He invented machinery for plowing the earth and harvesting crops. He also discovered methods for storage of crops and different ways of cooking food and the man came up with a lesson and ablation technique to remove barley and wheat from their husks. Then milled it with the help using a mortar or mill which then invents methods to transform flour into flakes, and later was aware of the importance of yeast. It is a marvellous way the flour flakes are transformed into a bread that pops when cooked in a specially-designed oven was designed for this purpose. When the man became herder, he changed into a shepherd after he began domesticating the animal in order to control the animal, since agriculture was concerned about the mirror. However, the shepherd was not the one who had the primary role in agriculture was not a woman. The majority of living things was the result of the woman, therefore even the gods who were associated with agriculture were female.

The most significant revolution known to man occurred when man was transformed from being a creature who lived as a guest in nature to fulfill his desire to eat by eating the fruit from the soil and hunting to one who produces his strength, after he was introduced to the cultivation of crops and methods for domesticating animals. The revolution in agriculture led to civilization, or the constant stable human population. The population density grew a significant amount, allowing it to create a village, eventually a city, eventually, states that had unison sovereignty. The

The development of agriculture also led to food surpluses and the creation one of the first towns. This revolution is a manifestation of the state of mind where a person has mastered the cultivation and production of "food" and isn't content with just the collection of food or hunting for it. This means that food was the property of domestic livestock after having been naturally wild. If we were to pick the most significant and significant alteration that took place in human history until the present it would be the domestication and the domestication of food. It wasn't achieved until numerous events and unintentional actions, and was solely at the hands of those same peoples who lived through collecting and collecting. This is how the human being was liberated from one of the bonds that tie him to the natural world, and his release from the limitations of nature's resources for food.

Mining

The pursuit of man's discoveries never stopped after the time he was aware of and engaged in agriculture, however his enthusiasm for understanding his surroundings and the things it held and he began the exploration of minerals, specifically copper. He then added tin to it and tin, creating an alloy of bronze. The bronze artefacts changed and improved after people were taught how to make metals. Then, in the Iron Age, man discovered an entirely new mineral called iron. Iron was an entirely new discovery when it came to use. The method of casting iron is distinct from the process of melting copper, so it wasn't an inevitable stage in the manufacturing of bronze and copper. Minerals were essential to the opportunity to grow construction, agriculture industries and also helped to establish the foundations of ancient civilizations.

Chapter 2: Creation Of Language

The human ascendancy has gone through various stages , each with its own distinct developmental pattern that have led to his development of greater comprehension and communication. When the first man was able to convey his thoughts using movements and gestures, significant changes took place throughout human history. This was the creation that of the language to be a tool for communication, and the development of mishaps and the control of thought. The language - strictly speaking - is a cultural phenomenon, and consequently, it is a part of the human being that is equipped with language tools, is able to use perception, and has the mechanisms of language. Human language is a set of words that communicate information (abstractions) that are words transform into mental symbols that we employ.

There is a belief that what he employed were sounds with different tone and intensity, as being a mimic of animal sounds as a result of his various emotions to signify the incident. The phonetic language started with just a few words. Then he began writing with forms from nature. We don't fully recognize the efforts we've taken to master how to understand our own language as human beings as we only discuss the objects that are put inside our mouths to use. However, the words - in their true meaning - were likely to have come into existence at the exact time the first indications of culture were discovered, as the two are the same thing.

Writing was invented by the inventors of

Man was writing since 4th millennium BC and its methods and methods were diverse, and the writings also grew. The invention of writing marks an important step in the evolution of civilizations in the human story. Human ascendancy reached a peak when he began to learn to write and to transcribe; as every form of expression was given an entirely new form. The change in material was followed by an intellectual transformation that led to the shift of human perception of the world, to the new worldview that was which was characterized by a radical change in values, symbols and all of the thinking. He was familiar with Egyptian visual writing. If a person was knowledgeable about agriculture and was content in a certain degree that his basic needs would be met like drinking water, food, safe shelter, and clothing could be hid in winter ... The individual was able to relax and enjoy peace. Then, as the man started to consider and reflect using a simple thought process, but he soon began to expand and become more complicated and, over time, wrote down his ideas.

In reality, the invention of writing was more than an event in the evolutionary process of humanity. In addition, it can be stated it was a creation but rather an exploration of an archetype that was the first to be used as an expression. With it, man was transformed from an introspective about meaning to an open display of it and when he crossed this threshold, man had been completed as a psychological system. Writing is also the thing that invented and established the foundation to store memories and knowledge, and the dissemination of science and knowledge. The history of the world started with the practice of drawing in pictures. Cuneiform texts. These were the first writing systems.

Early models of the evolution of human thought

It was during the middle of the 1st millennium BC the first book was discovered in the the ancient India known as (The Veda) which translates to it was the Book of Knowledge, and it was a religious book with a wide range of philosophical views and thoughts concerning man's morality, man's morality and even the entire world.

The (Veda) was a sacred text until the sixth centuries B.C., and the rise of (Jainism), meaning the victors, with the aim of teaching methods of liberating our souls from excessive desires that are caused by the ignorance of the world. In the fifth and sixth millennia BC, (Buddhism) appeared with the major topics focused on the fact that life is a constant struggle and suffering, and that there are reasons behind the appearance of torture and there is a way to alleviate the pain. The aim of learning in Buddhism is to free one of their suffering and pain. Then Buddhism was followed by the spread of yoga which is a form of meditation or focusing on oneself and freedom from the fetters that bind us to the outside world. The aim is to free oneself of suffering and ultimately, salvation is obtained through abstinence as well as adherence to high-value ethical principles.

If that is the case, then it is the nature of Indian thoughts at the time. It is evident that there was an amazing and massive development in the thinking of the Egyptians and the Babylonians. The growth of agriculture demanded expanding the knowledge circle for its application in the real world. In order to determine the amount of Nile river, science called astronomy was developed in the Egyptians and they made notable successes in the area of mathematics. They also calculated the duration of the year in three quarters of 365 days. Pharaonic literary effect reveals that living creatures are created from cold water. They also say that the air fills up the space and is found everywhere. It was believed that the Egyptians are farmers and which is why they had a lot of experience in the field of astronomy which allowed them to predict the flooding in the Nile. It was the Egyptian priests also taught writing using images.

In Babylon and during the 3rd century B.C., we find that the Babylonians set the foundations for geometry and algebra, and created a calendar based upon keeping track of the movements of the moon, sun and the stars. They created the sixty system for calculations, which is used to this day in which they split the hour into sixty minutes into minutes sixty seconds. Sumerians were also well-known for their cuneiform writing. Then they ate the vast empires of the Highness which centered their attention on happiness in the world. To achieve this, they tended to record the motions of the stars, and used magic and astrology.

In Chinese philosophy, another change occurred, and the doctrines of Confucius were revealed as well as the Confucian school believed that fate is the main factor that determines the lives of people like how individuals, by their education are distinguished. the old should be studied in order to be able to discern the truth of the.

The Greeks benefitted in Babylon, Iran, Egypt and Phenicia in a variety of areas, like geography, mathematics, astronomy measurement and evaluation. In the sixth and seventh millennia BC, Greek thinkers appeared and set out to search for the root of the universe.

In what manners or approaches did they attempt to determine the earliest causes?

From the 11th century BC there was a settlement called (Iona) The colony is regarded as to be the first cradle of

Coast philosophy is situated at the center of western region of Asia Minor. The population of the island has risen into the adjacent Aegean islands. There , the poet (Homer) was famous for his belief that human beings are comprised of body and soul and that the body is composed of dust and water. The body disintegrates when it dies, whereas the soul is comfortable air that springs from from the body, preserving its feelings.

Then after Hieromus was (Thales) the last of seven wise people who attempted to change morals and systems. He traveled to Egypt and learned the science of engineering from the scientists and created a hypothesis that states: Water is the primary element in all of the Universe ... And that everything was created from water. It was believed by him that magnets possess a soul since they can move iron. He predicted an eclipse of the sun in 585 BC. Based on the observatory observations regarding the Phoenicians regarding the periodic movement of the eclipse.

Then we discover that (Anximander) views that the Earth like a circular object that is floating with no chains, and the human being is at an end. He also has a person who requires in his early years an extended period of care and is grounded in the sea fish He also suggests that we not eat our fish-loving brothers. In the case of Pythagoras as well as his institution, we can see that they contributed to the development of a mathematical and scientific heritage , in particular. Pythagoras was the first to discover the basic numerical relation of what's known as musical distances and the Pythagorean concept states that everything is a number and to comprehend the world, we need to know the numbers in all things. He came across the right-angled triangle concept, that derived its fundamentals from Ancient Egyptians and

Babylonians who received engineering sciences from the hands of their masters, to grasp this theory it .was required to locate an explanation in deaf numbers

About 3500 BC. The most significant

The transformation of the intellectual world was witnessed after the advent of agriculture about five thousand years ago. This was the total revolution in civilization in Mesopotamia with a huge potential for production. It created vast communities in those of the Tigris as well as the Euphrates rivers. In Egypt the ancient civilization was founded in the delta that ran along the Nile River. It was the time of irrigation systems. This set the stage for the urban revolution with a variety of technological advancements within the agriculture community. The power of oxens and wind, plows, canoe and cart was harnessed. When man began to discover the properties of the metals, he was taught about copper .and bronze melting

Civil society also highlighted the accomplishments of ancient civilizations, like the building of monumental structures ... Pyramids statues, temples and pyramids. Civilization also needed laws that regulate the lives of people and provides them with greater security so that they can contemplate the future and strive to realize their human potential through the artistic possibilities that are provided through diversity. Additionally, it needed other ways of communication, which eventually resulted in the development of writing and its .diversity printing and its evolution

The most stunning and beautiful aspects that the writing process has accomplished is that it has created the written record that aids in the growth of civilizations and allowed generations to begin at the point where the preceding ones were, trying to improve the present life. The way that culture was practiced was once oral, before the advent of writing. It was based on the memories of the old to pass stories of their own stories across generations. They would remember what they had said and repeat it repeatedly like other nations before them. The benefit of memorizing was appreciated by a few and absorbed within their minds. They formed a group comprising historians, priests, singers and poets The tales, facts and the history of nations were written down in their memory up to the .era of writing.

Through writing or recording one does not have to store everything that is in their memory susceptible to death and forgetfulness or the memories the goals, intentions and goals of the person telling the story of what was happening in the past generation. Through writing, the mind became conscious of different interpretations, and the capacity to grasp the meaning of inner things. This understanding of the diversity of things can lead to opportunities for criticism, analysis , and authorship. The art of writing was able to be flexible following the year 2000 BC. The phonemic pronunciation gradually replaced the use of figurative writing in business. Phonemic writing systems are more straightforward and less symbolic. This resulted in a sophisticated system of puns that are visual. This revolution in the field of writing led to the entrance of huge number of people to participate, and resulted in a variety of thought and innovative styles.

Thus, culture encompasses memorization and knowledge of things, the capacity to make different points of view as well as the capacity to discover multiple meanings for things. This is exactly what led those who were Sophists as well as Manifesto teachers to overstate the diversity of opinions at the beginning.

The lullabies of some people

Man, in the face of the challenges and obstacles of nature began to develop and even created illusions created by those who have strayed to the edge of despair, following the arduous struggle which was ineffective. or people who were dissatisfied with their lives, and would rather blame their failures on the shoulders of the other or felt they could pass their burdens to the people who think that he will be able to save them from the mistakes they'd committed. Each day has its own fantasies that people create.

Chapter 3: "Philophers And Sophists"

The word "sophistry" was originally used to refer to instructors of this statement as well as teachers who teach wisdom from diverse areas. The meaning changed to the fallacies of instructors in the art of fallacy. Following the time that Athena beat his enemies the Persians as well as defeated the Persians, poets, scholars doctors, craftsmen and scholars excelled in their work. Political pluralism was enhanced as competition grew between individuals and the causes of conflict became more frequent before courts as political and judicial controversy was abound, which led to the need to study techniques of argumentation and rhetoric and also enticed people. A group of gifted individuals saw an opportunity to use their talents in Bayan's teachers. Bayan's instructors.

At the end of fifth century BC In the fifth century BC, an entire set of educators (teachers of the assertion) came to Athens (or the wisemen) across all directions regardless of the various areas of science or in the education of craft or other useful professions. Another change occurred when teachers who were known as"fallacies" and "teachers of fallacy as well as verbal games emerged. The reason is that sophists, or speech specialists can be the very first people to learn wisdom and the art of rhetoric in the pursuit of material gain.

Different types of teachers began to show up, for example, there were a group comprising teachers that were teaching rhetoric, literature, eloquence, and rhetoric, as well as managing the affairs of the political councils. Teachers of another kind instruct on debate and controversy, because they could teach the basic principles of argument and discourse before the courts for those who wanted to defend themselves and others.

Regarding the thoughts of the philosophers, they denied that they could know the truth. They rejected philosophy, and were against ideologies against each other. They asking people to think about reasoning and truth and shattered the rules to distinguish good from injustice and evil and also said that anything is possible to prove or disproved, and knowledge has evolved into Relativism Morality is a relative concept and good is a relative concept .. The use of language and games has replaced rational scientific thinking. They are subject to methodologies of scientific methodology as well as research conducted in science subject to the rules and instruments of scientific understanding.

Socrates is regarded as the most brilliant philosopher Athena has ever met during the 5th century B.C. Socrates the father of philosophers was always thinking ... at peace with his talkative wife , who controlled him and was patient with his fellow citizens because of their lack of knowledge. Socrates's thinking was centered on the human condition and his issues. Socrates was always adroit in getting every person who came across him to inquire about the subjects which occupied him, and then pretending to be ignorant and seeking out knowledge from other people. The way he approached his work was two-fold of sarcasm and asking and procreation. He helped others get information from their minds and minds.

Socrates is of the opinion that man is born with both a mind and a sense however, it is the mind that governs the senses, as all lawful laws that correspond to the real human condition are typically formulated by the mind. It is a type of laws that God created on the minds of the people .. That's why everyone is committed to observing just laws. It is true that it follows God's divine law and the mind. If anyone is attempting to defy it, is going to be punished in this life and, if not punished here in this life justice will be dealt into consideration in the following life. Socrates says that an individual who is healthy always seeks to be good and necessarily avoids evil.

Socrates has his famous cry that reads:"O man, be aware of yourself. Anyone who has his characteristics is healthy or always looking for good, or is lustful. A healthy person is the one who is seeking good and avoids evil in the end, and one who is clear on what is important and is aware of the good things will certainly desire it. In the case of Al-Shahwani is a person who is ignorant of himself and his good character as it is unjust to do evil. So it is a science to study virtue and vice .ignorance

Socrates was a devoted patriot, who was not difficult to find ... also was a courageous and trustworthy soldier. He fought in two wars. He was a prominent senator in the Senate and was well-known for his honesty and a diversity of thought among Democrats. He returned to his former time of research and guidance at the end of his tenure as a member of the Senate. A large number of young people were gathered around him, which included wealthy men such as Plato and generals of the army such as the Cebades and the general Socrates was the one who saved him during an earlier battle and the crowds who gathered around him, invited to eat at their tables, and enjoyed his denigration on the democracy of Athens. The priest said to him that Socrates controlled all of Greece and explained this claim by the Agnosticism that was the genesis of his philosophy and in which he said"I know only one thing, that is I don't know anything.

It is within her shadow that people can rise and thrive. Socrates was the one to take the poison cup from the hands of the prisoner who was grieving over him. He accepted the drink in a simple and gentle manner, and then placed it on his lips with peace and happiness. And Plato states: When I was crying We were then rebuked, and asked to go to sleep peacefully, stay peaceful and patient. This was the end of the story of what Plato described as ..."the most wise fairest, most beautiful, and the best of the men I've met in my life. Because of Socrates the philosophy shifted from the cosmology of ancient times to the study of anthropology. Socrates was determined to liberate man from the bonds he had to other people and his sinister desires.

and Socrates believed in a single God and that death is not the end of the story, and that there should exist an eternal moral law and it shouldn't base itself on a faith less tolerant than the religion of both. Socrates was accused of having a hand in provoking the general El Sebades, against the state and was brought to an indictment. .He was adamant that the rulers must be aristocratic.

Socrates defends his rights as a human being and the free flow of his thought. Athena's democratic system has written in its superficiality the name of Socrates, the first philosopher to die who refused to beg for mercy from those who would have freed him had he done. Socrates was imprisoned to prepare for execution therefore his followers gathered and formulated the rationale for his escape, however Socrates was not willing to break rules of the nation even though he was ruled in a dark way, despite the laws. He declared: Laws constitute the boundary of the state.

Plato's contribution to the human mind:

Plato was a pupil of Socrates. Plato's encounter in the company of Socrates was a pivotal event to his entire life. He's a rich young man, who was raised in an environment of comfort. Plato was born in Athens to an established family that was able to handle an abundance of ethnic tensions. He was exposed to various theories during his time. When he was twenty-something, he became acquainted with Socrates and began to study with him as well as benefitted from the many trips , which included a visit to Egypt. Plato was enthralled by playing with his teacher Socrates and this one-sided dialectical logic, and was intrigued by the way Socrates challenge the old proofs and theories and flip theories upside down. Plato began playing this game and moved from one stage to another thanks to his teacher Socrates as well as from mere discussion to precise analysis and productive conversations. Plato became passionate about the art of learning and his teacher, Socrates.

Plato was aware that - due to the events that he witnessed during his time and location - that a fair government will not get pardoned and must be prepared with education. This was among the main reasons that led him to create his academy near the gates of Athens and the academy was the basis of the universities that grew later. Plato established his school as an association of scholars and religious leaders and remarked on it, "No sign written on it. Only philosophers and engineers is allowed to attend the academy and Plato forbids anyone who wants to attend ".it without being an expert in math

And Plato wrote and taught in the Academy over forty years. It lasted for nine hundred years before it was shut down in the 6th century AD. The school's founders left to Persia and, from there, the Greek philosophy was spread towards the East and then made its route to Arabs who developed and grafted it onto Islamic dye, and then translated to .Latin and then transferred it to Europe

The academy of this time Plato was in charge of the instruction of all branches of knowledge. He created specialized teachers for each branch and was in the forefront of these schools in the field. Plato continued to devote the remainder of his time thinking about the subject of governance and the traits of those who he deemed to be his favored as a ruler.

He is a judge of the law and doesn't make mistakes. Plato was always looking for a great ruler or a person competent enough to make justice. In his time of teaching the young ruler of Athens the importance of justice, the ruler became angry and ordered Plato to go to auction at the slave market. So someone who was impressed with his ideas took him in and bought him a house. an area to contemplate. In addition, Plato thought that philosophers were the most important of all people.

They are the top of their kind due because of their thirst for knowledge and their rich culture. He believes that a philosopher is one who is devoted to learning and wisdom, is influenced by it, believes in the truth and reaches beyond the world of phenomena to their own innermost being. This .person is deserving of being judged.

The principle that Plato's philosophy was based on is the notion of having a suitable ruler within the realm of utopia. According to Plato the state cannot be considered legitimate unless it is run by a philosopher. He also believed the ruler has to have studied philosophy so that the republic, or utopia is possible. He believes that all studies is subordinate to rules of discussion (passing through both ascending and decresing debate) and that this can only be recognized by the mind of the individual. In this manner, Plato adopted the technique of dialogue when he wrote the majority of his writings, being inspired by his teacher, Socrates and also influenced by the theatre that was popular at the period. Plato's knowledge of the importance of education was the fact that he believed that the goal of education isn't to overwhelm students with the greatest number of facts. It is more important to provide the necessary syllabus, and put the learning to the examination. It's this type of .organization that could quickly eliminate the sophist's idea of truth.

Plato is of the opinion that senses can only be transferred to us by flimsy memories of things we can recognize. And that the reality that has changed is only perceived by the eyes of our minds. Within the mind are the essential meanings that we need to evaluate the material. Like there are over the mind and beyond the body, there exist abstract beings we refer to as forms. Every body has an analogy to. Forms are made up of the physical world and forms are made up of the rational universe, similar to how the world of the body is derived out of the universe made up of shapes ... The actual existence is that of the forms. Things and bodies are just shadows and ghosts from this reality. It is believed that the soul was close to the ideals before it entered the world of this, and our real understanding of the world is based on recalling the ideals through tangible things. The thing you see in the world is just a representation of the original example and that its existence is only apparent, and it is a reflection of the reality.

So, it is concluded that existence is composed of two parts that are a sensory perception that is perceived by the senses and a mental one that is only perceived through the brain. The perception of sensual existence includes two components The first is the actual object and the other is the image of it. Based on this view we discover that Plato's philosophy of knowledge is linked to his conception of the world. He also believes that art is an imitation of simulation and he was against accepting poets to his ideal city. Even though there was a poet. The soul's mother According to Plato was a former existence in the realm of forms before being trapped in the body while the soul, according to Plato is eternal due to its divine nature. Plato's theories, which shaped an important legacy for the future.

Plato was a descendant of his predecessors in the group of seven wise men. They are these wise men, who are not well-known about other than the wise man Solon or Solon who was from Athens and was the Greek writer and politician. He was one of the greatest politicians. Also, the citizens of Athens chose him to be their ruler who lived in the 6th and 7th centuries BC. He believed in the supremacy of law and believed that every group of citizens must abide by the law's provisions.

He was a descendant of the route taken by him to reach the utopian city he longed for and sought. The wise Khilion of Spartan among the

Greek philosophers from the sixth century BC and was appointed an observer from a group of five to the King of Sparta and also made changes regarding Spartan policies that resulted in an alliance with the Peloponnese later, and later became poet. The sage, known as the royal Thales lived between 640 and 546 BC. Thales was an Greek mathematician and astronomer as well as a philosopher of the Ionian School. Hakim Bayas from Priene, an Greek philosophy professor, was believed to be responsible for enacting social law following an armed struggle which was waged by the people of the poor against the angel class and their laws were known as Attica. The smart person Cleopoulos of Lindos is an important Greek philosophers from the sixth century BC and the reign of Sparta in the early days of Greece. The Sage Petacus of Mytilene was alive between 650 and the year 570 BC. He was the name of a Greek politician as well as a sage and was crowned ruler by the inhabitants in Mytilene at the time of 590 BC. In order to defend them from nobles who were exiled. Hakim Periander of Corinth, the second King of Corinth was a city that developed both socially and commercially

(627-586 BC). The Sage Homer is a renowned Greek epic poet. his dates of birth were the subject of debate throughout the classical period until today. It is not known with certainty.

One of Solon's main concerns was the administration elements of government which is why his laws were designed to controlling state employees in their work in the administrative sphere These laws were named in honor of Solon's laws and his view that of equality in society in a nation shattered by a rift between the wealthy and the poor. So Solon made the decision to pay off the debts of his

By limiting individual ownership of the land as well as the rights of peasants through the division of the land between them. Soloon also became interested in industrial arts and crafts, so the regulations he instituted to revive them. And his passion for crafts resulted from the necessity that the agriculture sector was no longer enough to satisfy the demands of the nation and create fields of employment and he realised that the wealthy grew up in a state of luxury and resentful extravagant lifestyle, and he passed laws that restricted these types of behavior. Solun is also acknowledged for abolishing slavery, which was the first constitutional change that was ever implemented in Greek history. Solun also secured the freedoms of the wage-earners and the common people and allowed them to participate in the electoral process. The law granted the participation in politics and government to ordinary citizens. He enacted several significant changes. He introduced modern social laws.

Chapter 4: Confucius In The Fifth Century Bc In China

According to Confucius during 5th century BC in China who was birthed in the year 551 BC. He was fascinated by how to conduct governance and believed that the possibility existed to attain the model of good governance through the application of his instructions, and then looking for a trustworthy ruler who would grant him the authority to change society. Confucius identified the government's purpose and its role in achieving three goals to ensure that people have enough food and water, adequate weapons, and trust in their leader. Humanism is the Confucian concept of what a socially acceptable society should look like. By focusing on 3 axes: ethics education, and politics.

The role that was played by Confucius was crucial to the transformation of the old Chinese society. It is this role that brings humanity back to the individual and ensures his morality. He connected his teachings to happiness for humans. Therefore, it seems that the human mind is linked to the reality of society from the context from which it was born. The individual who thinks isn't isolated from his community or the issues and conditions of his day and life, but is a part of the whole and interacts with it. This is the reason Confucius discussed the practice of

Should judgment be made be taken into account, and believes that the right people (and not other people) should be entrusted with the administration of the state and that this can only accomplished if the decision is legitimate.

The author believes that a successful ministry has responsibilities that it must complete, including the following: The primary task for the minister is to achieve self-sufficiency as well as distribute wealth to the masses on the biggest scale. The second goal is to develop non-harsh laws in order to lessen punishment. The third objective is to increase education with the goal to improve the standard of the citizens. And education is not complete without supplements, which includes the inculcation of moral values and behavior. All that contributes to .the happiness of the country

As well as from the ongoing episodes that have shaped the intellectual growth of mankind. One of the pioneers of Greek thinking and humanity generally and the early teacher Aristotle Thales, and the Arab philosophers, who called Al-Hakim as well. he was known throughout the West as the philosopher, or prince of philosophers, and the master of knowledge. His philosophy has been the dominant force in the human mind for more than 2 millennia. It is a philosophy that has influenced both the East as well as West together. The issues raised by Aristotle following the steps of his mentor, Plato, were and are the main mental challenges. The approach created by Plato in the dialogue was further refined by Aristotle and finally reached perfect.

Aristotle was interested in the issues that should be available for the management of the government's affairs. He believed that a country where the middle class is dominant is the most stable and stable of nations. It emphasizes the importance of family as the child is under the supervision of his parents, which limit the amount of responsibility that, when given to the society at large can lead to abandonment. The state was described by Aristotle as a structure that blends with a certain degree of various interests. Aristotle considered the economic aspect to be of significant importance in the .state

With the assistance by Alexander, Aristotle was able to establish the first zoo that was known to humans. This garden was utilized for his research and experiments with animals and plants. Additionally, Aristotle was capable of establishing an embryology. In which he followed the model of Hippocrates and conducted research which allowed him to explain the evolution of thieves which has enthralled embryologists to the present. Aristotle also defined what he considered to be the ideal man, which he stated, is the one who is not willing to take risks that are not necessary and is willing to risk his life when faced with a crisis. It also helps people and to benefit them

He avoids boasting and faking. And he is open about his opinions, hatreds or words, as well as deeds. He is not afflicted by hate or prejudice He is also able to forget and forgive offenses and has a small amount of conversation and also talk about people even when they are enemies of his He is not hasty or hasty. He does not fear being lonely and is the most loyal person to be with is himself. He created his School of Luqion at the 335 BC.

The book he wrote was titled "Natural Listening" where the issue of movement was discussed. It contained lectures on physics, which is, on the natural sciences that he taught his students. It is his most important textbook on Physics. This publication "Post-Nature" has been written by Aristotle as he was advancing in his spiritual and intellectual development. The book addresses the issue of movement. The first article in Natural Audiology was on the nature of the natural sciences and their methodological approach. The second article was on nature (that is the subject to nature, or science that studies nature). He stated that the assets of nature are the ones that are in nature, while some are derived from different factors. The third article dealt with motion and the definition of it. The fourth article discussed the importance of understanding the location it is located, its definition and challenges surrounding it, as well as the examination of the words spoken in the past and in its definition as well as the present, past and future of it. The fifth article dealt with fundamental distinctions for studying the movements and their surroundings. The sixth article was about investigating the structure for the contactor (the caller and the encounter and the next) along with (time and grandeur) as well as (movement as well as stillness within the current) and (the separation of the elements that constitute motion) and (the beginning phases of transformation) as well ... and..etc .. Seventh article speaks about the evidence for the existence of the first mover.

The principle behind the attic motor and motile. It is believed that the change takes place in accordance with sensor data, contrast between the motions, and the fundamental equations in the field of dynamics. In the eighth article , he discussed the origins of movement as well as the development of the first engines.

Aristotle advocated equality and justice for everyone. and rebalance by his moral convictions. He looked over the various constitutions, including the idea that the most effective constitution is one where wealth is not excessive and scarce. It is essential that the size of the state should be proportional to its population.

and to possess the required capabilities. I believe that a good system of governance is one where there is no chance of using power for ruler's personal gain. Furthermore, Aristotle declares that the political system is not a place where people are made. You must consider the natural circumstances of people. Aristotle was an unassuming, skeptical philosopher, who focused his thought process on the application of logic. Also, he believed in it was a believer in extrapolation. He believed in the ability of our minds to gain access information. The foundation of this belief was sciences and physics. And in this regard the state is been a result of the development of history and has been through various social levels before reaching that state level. Aristotle is the third of the greatest thinkers who resided in Athens. At the end of his life Aristotle was accused of being against the dominant faith and was banished from Athens. The ideas of Aristotle are many including in logic, philosophy and nature, as well as in poetry, politics, as well as ethics.

Human thinking during the Hellenistic period or Hellenistic Roman time period:

The end of the 5th century BC, Sparta besieged and defeated Athens and thus shifted over the political power of Athens as the home of Greek philosophy and art, leading to the decline of the arts and culture as well as the autonomy from The Athenian mind. Also, the appearance of Alexander the Great in Macedonia was the first time that Macedonia had control over that country , first militarily and later politically and the society was transformed and the ruling families were forged until the end of the century, and following which was and came the Roman Empire in which a handful of rulers, who had were able to develop themselves in stages, reformed and redesigned their ways of governance, and established the social structure that was common to all Western civilization, and for this, they were able to remain in power for a lengthy period of.

And the awe-inspiring influence that Aristotle and the philosophy of Macedon in the field of Greek philosophy shows the political surrender that was the norm in Greece in the face of the young brave people from the North. Alexander's death has accelerated the process of Greek decline. Alexander's life Alexander is the key event in the course of human historical. Alexander is thought to have been in the middle of the engineering field of human development. the human experience after his death is quite different from

journey. Human life is ahead of him, as though it were somewhere in the middle of all humanity's Furthermore, his field of work is situated within the middle of the globe in the way he imagined it. Alexander was able to achieve his goals through the interplay of military victories with a sound political system, art trade, as well as technological and scientific advancement. He was born when he was twenty , and lived to . .his death at the age of 33 on the 28th of June 323 BC

In this time, different there are different mentalities are being developed, other than the Greek mentality are being explored.

Then, it was apparent that there was a difference between it was the Roman mentality as well as the Eastern mentality. This era was triggered by the demise of Aristotle. The era started after his death in Alexander the Great in 323 BC. It is believed that the phrase Hellenistic can be used to differentiate this time period with earlier periods. Hellenistic time period. This was the time when the ancient Greeks under the empire of the ethnic. In the course of time, Greek culture spread throughout the nations of the East there was a marriage of Greek cultural traditions and Eastern culture. Both was influenced in a way by another. Philosophical thought was centered on ethics and was is influenced by mysticism and religion.

In fact, several philosophical schools of philosophy were created.

The most significant school of Hellenistic philosophy include that of Stoics, Epicureans, Cynics and Neoplatonism. The philosophy in the Stoic and Epicurean schools was saturated by morals, and the Cynics attempted to .overlook the pleasures and desires of all kinds and seek out morality

The philosophy of the past was infused within those schools like Epicureanism and Neoplatonism by mysticism and religion. These schools had many of their inspirations from the earlier philosophers, particularly Plato and Aristotle and incorporated into the other elements of philosophy. In the expansion of Roman Empire opened all avenues for the movement to the migration of Eastern populations to Europe. They developed ideas and art and then began speaking the Greek language, and later Latin and later began to establish new religions which led to the conversion of educated people from the Roman Empire and following them, their kings of honor, to new religions that value human rights, preaches equality and co-existence among human beings and opposes .the dependence of man on the other man.

The fall of the Roman Empire was followed by states who considered themselves to be as the protectors for Western civilization. Then, modern European society was born after a number of radical shifts in the way of thinking and activity. These changes caused social tensions along with political revolutions. Regarding it was the Hellenic revolution. Alexander was planning to rule all of the world to enrich the world, making it more enlightened and linking it by building cities. And the aim of building these cities was to provide a place of meeting for all civilizations and gatherings of cultures and peoples. Also, to provide a area of stability for different kinds of trade, different types of industries, and craftsmen who come from a variety of nations, spoke different .Sunnis and belonged to various nationalities.

When people move into these cities to live permanently and live permanently, they are treated exactly in the same way, without distinction in any way. So, the civilization rises to a new stage which is more interconnected and complex. The cities develop into organizations of high production, advanced education, high-culture and the creation of a new society. Thus, the construction of a new city took place with a fluidity during the reign of Alexander the Great and his successors strategically located along the route of caravans, either on internal roads or coastal roads. The book examines the development in Greek culture in language, literature and science, as well as the arts, history as well as philosophy, religion and in the administration of the government as well as in conflict (as . (performers

The expansion of these cultures following the victory by Alexander the Great is among the most clear examples of history. Alexander established an organization to oversee the management of the empire. He also introduced ideas and technology from the Greeks. Greek ideas and ideas as well as the principles of as law, governance as well as methods of colonization and methods of trade as well as methods of colonization, law, and trade. Greeks created and refined these, and then the time their successors .came and adopted them

The world's ideas were liberated when they learned how to speak Greek within the Hellenistic world. Despite the fact that there was never a gathering between the various classes of society in which races were split. The spreading of Hellenism had the effect of freeing human thought from prior restrictions which was obvious in the ethical dimension that the Stoics were at the top of and continue to feed our thinking into the present day. Since the beginning of time, humans have been aware of the distinct distinctions in mental capacity and the capacity of muscles among different individuals However, during the Hellenistic time and later, people like the Greeks and Jews were able to formulate ideas calling to accept these distinctions and an attempt at be equal between all people. Christianity as well as Islam began to endorse the concept of equality.

However, it was Hellenism who created the equality between men. In the period that of Alexander the Great The Greek world was on the offensive phase and the entire world was subject to within a short amount of time, one ruler Alexander. Absolutely, the Macedonian victory was more successful as an exemplar to Greek influences. It brought the Greek civilization and spread it across Asia. The East brought a new effect on West. The concept of specialization is becoming more popular. The experts from that Hellenistic world were limited to a specific area. At the end of this golden age city-states and the Greek world was struck by a decrease in its vitality and vitality. One could say that the demise of Socrates was the turning point within Greek culture. As we sank into the valleys that comprised Hellenistic cultural ethos, a myriad of new concepts started to emerge in the field of the field of philosophy. Overall: since the topic is vast. it is possible to say . Each scholar of thought - throughout the history of human thinking - has a relation to other thought leaders. When he learns or absorbs their thoughts and assimilates it, the process that are a battle between ideas of his predecessors and, after wrestling with himand develops his understanding and appreciation of important issues and issues, he starts his own approach to the issues in a manner that is compatible and in keeping with the conditions of his day and the environment where he is and is in accordance with the ideas of those who took their inspiration from all of their thinking. His thinking is a reflection of the sources and origins the thought he came from, whether that was art, religion, literature or mythology or any field of study. They are part of the realm of reasoning. Who shaped and influenced the human mind. Also, thought and its development are a part of time and within. This means the fact that human beings are intellectual. Indeed man is the subject of all science whether in a direct or indirect way. This is the reason we attempt to study the following areas to study the subject from various angles and hoping to impart some insight. Follow us. The next one is even more stunning.

A closing word

The trace of the steps man made before the beginning of time in order to open the way for the civilization that has been a part of history. To help us understand the phases of development of events that helped the man of the jungle or the caveman grow into the Egyptian architect or the Babylonian astronomer as well as the Hebrew prophet of the Hebrew prophet, the Persian ruler as well as the Greek poet or Roman engineer or the Indian saint and the Japanese artist or the Chinese Sage . Man has led an erratic life for the duration of the history of our time in search of food and sustenance until he is able to control and manage food. This has made it simpler for him to be part of tribes that live in stable villages. In addition, he came up with ways and ways to strengthen social ties. At the time of Bronze Age, people were in a position to form large groups in cities to prepare for the creation of states. This was achieved by advancing agricultural practices and food sources, and was assisted by the use of animals for strength and food. The first pioneers of thought-leaders continued to refine and polish the rough diamond's surface that symbolizes human existence and the challenges of nature to build new civilizations. Thus, we have to examine the way we perceive human medicine by looking at evolution.

What we know about human beings is a bit limited to the knowledge we have about other aspects of our natural and physical world. These stages must be addressed in the next independent topic, and, in the following attempts to be able to and even present the simplest summary of these phases to ensure we are as informed as much as we can. Keep us in mind and send the best of greetings to all our readers.

Chapter 5: The First Hominin Australopithecus

The name 'Australopithecus' for the genus is Latin meaning "Southern Ape" which signifies the fact that the first fossils belonging to the genus were discovered throughout the Southern regions of Africa. The first fossils found of Australopithecus are believed to be between 4.4 to 3.5 millions of years old. The genus remains on fossil records for a staggering 2 million more years. Over the course of time, various species were found within the genus. They were often co-existing with each other and new species emerging from earlier ones.

The fossils found in Australopithecus are sufficiently extensive to allow for a variety of general conclusions about the genus in general. One interesting aspect of Australopithecus is the fact that the diverse species don't tend to display a gradual progression of physical attributes, but rather appear to be a random collection of adaptations. Certain species were able to achieve upright walking, yet had not developed hand dexterity. While others had advanced grips, but maintained the posture of an ape.

The genus is an attempt at disorganization to explore every strategy to survive in an extremely harsh and constantly changing world. Differently distributed geographically across different environments and climates Each species came up with their individual strategies of adaptation that are best suited for their particular environment. In the course of time, segregated populations likely would have come into contact with each other, interbred , and brought together their unique traits. The traits that were more beneficial to physical health could be retained by the individuals with them, and they were more likely to live and reproduce. Certain of these "new and improved' people could establish the foundations for creation of a new species.

Although fossils found in Australopithecus may not be rare however they are not uncommon, nor are fossils found in hippopotamus and water buffalo of the exact same period. This is the case for all hominin species across time, because up until recently, hominins weren't a particularly flourishing evolutionary line, being mostly as small isolated populations. There are plenty of evidence to differentiate between the many types and kinds of Australopithecus.

The Artistic Concept of Appearance of Australopithecus Based upon fossil evidence.

Based on the fossil evidence we have discovered so far, it is conclusively concluded that there were two main categories of Australopithecus and both appear to include several species. There were two classes of Australopithecus, called the 'gracile' species as well as the species known as the 'robust. The names suggest that one group comprised smaller and lighter individuals, while the second comprised of larger and more bulky individuals. It is likely that these two groups represent two huge geographically separated populations that share one common ancestor, which later evolved in different ways like humans and Chimps.

The first finds of Australopithecus were discovered in around 1900. When more fossils were found, the hominins were assigned many classification names like Paranthropus, Ardipithecus, Kenyanthropus, Sahelanthropus, Cyphanthropus, Africanthropus, Telanthropus, Atlanthropus, Arambourg and Tchadanthropus. The paleoanthropologists soon concluded that they were probably somewhat overly enthusiastic when they associated the genus's name to every new discovery and that the entire collection likely belonged to one genus that was selected eventually as Australopithecus. The species known as 'robust' are still called Paranthropus. Because there isn't any complete DNA from fossils from the past and the fossils found are comparatively scarce so we'll probably never know whether the 'gracilis' and the 'robustus' were part of the same species or not. However, both species are usually not believed by paleoanthropologists to belong to the Genus Australopithecus and there isn't any convincing evidence to the contrary.

Possible appearance of a gracile (left) and robust (right) Australopithecus

Australopithecus seems to be evolving within East Africa. Then they expanded across the African continent in the course of time. The entire Australopithecus species were tiny in comparison to modern standards, with a body that was about the size of a modern chimp. Also, their brains were smaller than that of modern humans. It's possible that their behavior was similar to the Chimps. However, there are clearly notable differences between Australopithecus species, as well as modern Chimpanzees. For Australopithecus was an animal that was bipedal and walked on the ground.

The legs and arms of the diverse Australopithecus species still retained their strong climbing capabilities even though they may have all had climbed a tree quickly if they were feeling at risk, the fossils of arm and leg bones from Australopithecus certainly indicate that they were walking across the floor. More importantly they were walking on two legs. This is not surprising since when chimps and gorillas walk on four legs in the air, their close-related Asian counterpart, the orangutan, prefers to walk on two legs. The first evidence conclusive to prove that the earliest predecessors of ours were walking on two legs comes in the form of fossilized footprints. They were discovered at Laetoli within Tanzania and were found to be 3.6 million years old. The gate for walking is bipedal. The footprints of the feet look to be quite contemporary.

Image of Fossilized Footprints discovered within Tanzania (left) as well as also an artistic Impression from the Australopithecus Family Passing By Who Created Them (right)

There are some additional observations that we can draw from the physiology and health of Australopithecus as a whole. Australopithecus have bigger canine teeth in relation to body size than humans today, but not as big as modern Chimpanzees. So the common ancestor had smaller canines, and chimpanzees are now acquiring these teeth or Australopithecus canines have decreased in size. We aren't sure of the way that this took place. We do know that the large size of canines in hominids are usually connected to competition between males for females' access. Some males have a large share of females within chimps. Humans tend to reproduce in pairs. So it is likely that Australopithecus were mated in groups in between, with several females in one large family, partnered with a powerful male. It's all speculation because we don't have particulars of how the first hominins were living.

Canines of an Modern Chimpanzee. Very frightening.

To allow for erect walking, other changes were made to the legs, feet and the spine of Australopithecus. Chimpanzees have a big toe that can be pushed back to aid climbing trees by generating an grabbing motion like our hands. Australopithecus in contrast, and like us, has large toes that face toward the forward direction to assist in walking. The remaining toes were tiny in size like ours, which makes them better suited to walking rather instead of climbing. The bones of their legs are larger and straighter than those of the chimpanzee, however they are they aren't as long or straight as ours and suggest a move towards efficient walking.

It is believed that the knees of Australopithecus are also locked when standing, similar to ours, which reduces the stress that comes with standing for long durations. The same is true in herding animals, however it is it is not well-known among predatory animalsthat are more likely to lay down when they are not walking. This is not known to the tree-loving primates. Australopithecus has a slight S-curve in the spine like we do. This helps maintain the body's weight center over the hips during walking and standing postures. Similar to us, the pelvic bones of these animals were smaller than chimps and joined, providing structure to carry the body's weight when standing. Additionally their skulls were held by their spines, like ours, and not being extended forward from their bodies.

One question that needs to be considered at this time is: why would Australopithecus developed to move on only two feet instead of on four, when it was deprived of its forest habitat? Baboons, which is a monkey species who also lives on ground, walk on four feet. As we are all aware that almost all mammal species walk on 4 feet. This is due to the numerous advantages of walking on four legs over being straight or walking on two legs. To begin with, it can be seen if you've attempted to run faster than your dog legs are significantly quicker than two. Walking on four legs is also a more efficient way of walking, and requires less energy to cover the same distance when in comparison to standing. Being a prey to predators in the dirt, it doesn't make much sense to slow yourself down further by opting for walking with two legs instead of be able to run with four. What is the reason we chose to stand up?

Answers to this mystery can be found within the skull. Think of a cat that has four legs. The spinal cord enters the skull horizontally. It is what we think of as the back side of their heads. The entrance hole into the skull that is used for the spine is known as the 'foramen magnum'. Consider the human body. The spine is inserted vertically into the skull, through the skull's base. Any other orientation that is not horizontal or vertical isn't efficient for animals walking. A mammal is able to walk on four feet, and have the spinal cord enter through the back of the skull. Alternatively, they could walk on two feet, and have the spinal cord enter through the skull's base.

Animals that climb trees , however because of their incline position, usually have their vertebrae enter their skull approximately between the vertical and horizontal places. In general, the bigger the tree-living animal and the higher the tree's height, the more the position that the foramen magnum will tend to be inclined towards the vertical. For example, a squirrel is small , and therefore is able to have its spine enter the skull in the same way it would for a cat. However, an orangutan is larger. If the spine entered through the rear of the animal, the climb would be difficult. Therefore, the spine enters by a more diagonal direction.

The position of the Foramen Magnum in a Human (left) and the position of Foramen Magnum in a Wolf (right). Chimpanzees (middle) have a position closer to Humans.

If a tree-dwelling mammal had to fall to the ground and be forced to walk, it could choose between two options. The foramen magnum may change in time, allowing it to move towards the back of the skull. This animal may eventually walk on four legs effectively. The foramen magnum may shift towards the top of the skull and, eventually, mammals can effectively walk on two feet. For an animal of the large as a monkey the spine is further to the rear of the skull rather than at the top. Thus, pressures from the environment (i.e. for example, getting chased by hungry lions) can cause the evolution of foramen magnum taking it's position towards the back of the skull. This will allow the process of running away on four legs quicker for the monkey and increase the chances of not being consumed.

Imagine an animal that is the size of the chimpanzee. To climb upwards vertically on tree trunks, as the size of a chimpanzee it is best to adopt a bent hip and bent knee. This is better for back support and ensures a well-aligned centre of gravity. This type that tree climbers use is very similar to the Knuckle walking that is utilized by gorillas and chimps to walk in the earth. Due to this position, the spine is more at the bottom than the rear. Thus, if a chimp is forced to dwell at the foot, there would be an obstacle to the foramen magnum being moved towards the back of the skull in order to allow efficient walking on four legs. The issue could be that the animal might need to develop first in an inefficient orientation with a 45-degree angle between the front and the base of its skull.

It doesn't understand that if a creature could just go through this stage that is less able to survive, it will emerge as more able to survive at the final. The people born among our growing ground dwelling chimps that have spines entering the skull in an angle higher would be less efficient runners, and thus at a higher risk of being killed by predators. People born with spines that enter the skull closer to the base could be faster than normal chimps and thus more likely to live. According to the saying, when you are chased by bears it is not necessary to be more quickly than. Just run faster than the man next to you. So the common ancestor, who was once forced to live on the floor, had no other choice other than to develop into walking on two legs. So, Australopithecus stand erect.

The differences of Pelvis as well as Femur (Upper The Leg Bone) of the Chimp (left) in comparison to the Human (right). The Australopithecus was a transitional animal, but much closer to humans and fully capable of walking on two Legs efficiently, while the Chimpanzee isn't.

There were many important consequences that came from our forefathers becoming walkers with two legs. Primarily, hominins will never be speedy runners. We'd never be able to beat the majority of those who preyed upon us. Then our forward limbs were free. Our common ancestor was quite skilled hands to climb trees. These hands were now free to use for other reasons. Thus our ancestors of the past fated to walk on the earth with a the two legs and swaying arms without forests to give food and shelter were left with only a few options to them in order to survive. Actually, they had only one choice. Our ancestors were required to get more sophisticated. With those free hands, they needed to make use of their smarter brains to create tools.

Having reviewed the genus Australopithecus and its major physical characteristics, it is time to introduce each of the species of Australopithecus so far identified by paleoanthropologists. The species that are known to be the gracile Australopithecus comprise Australopithecus anamensis A. afarensis (The genus name is reduced by removing the first letter to reduce repeating), A. bahrelghazali, A. africanus, A. Garhi, as well as A. sediba. The species that are known to be part from the tough Australopithecus comprise A. Aethiopicus A. boisei, and A. robustus. The time-line relationship between the three species is illustrated in the chart below. The dates shown are approximate from fossil evidence that we have. It is important to note that time is older towards the right, which means that species appeared on the left of the chart only to disappeared towards the left.

The Timeline for each of the Australopithecus Species.

Map of fossil sites from earlier Australopithecus in Africa

All the species of gracile shared many characteristics. They had a look and size that was similar to chimpanzees, but they could walk with two legs , and with long , swinging arms. They were each about 1.2 up to 1.4 meters tall (4 up to 4.5 feet high). According to thermologic models (studies of loss of heat in the human body) It is believed that the Australopithecus species could have been completely covered with hairs on the body, similar to modern human chimps. The pelvis shape and feet was remarkably like those of humans of today, suggesting upright walking and a modern gait was already in place. The teeth from Australopithecus were tiny and had an extremely thick layer of enamel on their surfaces, which was much like human teeth, rather than Apes. A thick layer of enamel is vital when eating foods that are eaten in the ground instead of within trees to protect them of the dirt and grime that accompany the food items.

All Australopithecus graciles had 32 teeth, which is similar to chimpanzees as well as modern humans. The jaw's shape however has a form like modern humans and apes, as illustrated in the image below. While the molars in Apes are parallel to each their counterparts, they form the human jaw into a curvature. Australopithecus teeth were more parallel, indicating that the common ancestor had an arrangement. It is believed that it remains in the great Apes. The canines of the gracile Australopithecus however, are humans and apes in the size. The canines of apes are large and are used to fight among males to gain access to females and also in defense and attacking. The smaller canines of Australopithecus gracile suggest that they did not depend on the teeth to perform these functions.

The dentition in Chimp (Left), A. afarensis (middle) and Modern Humans (right). Notice the smaller Canines that belong to Australopithecus and Humans Comparing to Apes.

Molars from Australopithecus are arranged like they do in human with low crowns, and four cusps with rounded edges. This arrangement is perfect to crush tough plants. The cutting edges of the crests work well for cutting through meat. Based on this geometry of dentation, it is found that Australopithecus was gracile and consumed a mix of plant-based and animal products. The meat could have been gathered through hunts and the scavenging. Modern chimps will consume meat whenever it is available. They're both active hunters and can eat an unfinished carcass. It is thought that Australopithecus displayed similar behaviours. The wear patterns of their fossilized teeth suggest that the amount of vegetable matter Australopithecus consumed comprised fruits leaves, tubers, leaves seeds, and grasses.

The hands of the gracile Australopithecus were more apprehensive than humans, and were better suited for reaching trees and climbing than hand dexterity. With such hands, it is possible Australopithecus could make use of the same tools we now see human chimps employing. They would have hit nuts with stones and digging with sticks for termites, throwing bush to scare off predators and slashing small animals using sharpened sticks. Stones that are associated with Australopithecus indicate that they also had the capability of selecting natural-looking stones to use for specific uses for example, cutting through meat or smashing open bones.

The capability to break open bones with stone tools has given the gracile Australopithecus the capacity to gather an abundance of food which other animals would not be able to have access to. Inside bones is bone marrow, extremely rich in energy-rich fat. When a predator , such as the lion is killed by a large herding animal, they devour the carcass. Hyenas and jackals then enter the carcass and break open smaller bones using robust jaws. But Australopithecus could have visited the slaughter afterward and used large stones to break up the bigger bones that these animals couldn't break into. Small, simple stones that may serve this purpose were found in several locations in connection together with Australopithecus fossils, along with animal bones that showed evidence of being broken open.

It is also believed that the Australopithecus gracile employed wooden tools, but these aren't found in the archeological evidence. Simple sticks are a good option to dig tubers from the earth's hard surface. There's a bounty of nutrition that comes from the of the plant roots under the savannah's hard soil that can't be obtained without the use of tools. Access to abundant sources of energy through the use of a few tools like bones crushing stones and digging sticks could have been the basis of Australopithecus distinctive advantage for gathering food in comparison to other mammal species. These tools-based methods of gathering food would have offered all year round food sources that were not available to other species.

The first Australopithecus species with gracile gracile to be recorded in fossil records is A. Anamensis. It was from A. A. anamensis that other species of Australopithecus evolved. Fossils from A. Anamensis have been found to be at least 4.4 millennia ago. And the species remained alive until about 3.8 million years long ago. A. Anamensis is quite well-represented in fossil records, with more than 100 fossils discovered in more than twenty individuals. The fossils were found all over Kenya as well as Ethiopia. It is likely that the roots were located in East Africa, and that it was only later that the Australopithecus species moved further to and into the African continent.

These fossils from A. Anamensis consist of lower jaws, a portion from the jaw's upper teeth and skull fragments and parts of the lower and upper leg bones. While vast, these fossils are not a complete representation of the entire skeleton. Also, being derived from a variety of individuals over a long period of time, they do not accurately determine the physiology of this species. Even with this small amount of information, a pretty comprehensive comprehension of A. Anamensis is acquired. Even though it has a bipedal gait however, the upper limbs of A. Anamensis showed more resemblance to Chimpanzees than modern humans. It is believed that the species could climb trees in order to avoid predators, or to gain access to food when trees were readily available. It is believed that the majority of Australopithecus maintained this ability to climb trees effortlessly.

Australopithecus afarensis may be a descendant of A. Anamensis, and has fossils dating around 3.9 to 2.9 million years in the past. In order to put this in perspective, this species lived for a million years. Humans today are only couple of hundred thousand years. The most well-known hominin bones ever discovered was found to be a part of A. Afarensis. The skeleton was discovered by paleoanthropologist Donald Johanson and dated to 3.2 million years ago, the fossilized skeleton quickly gained the name 'Lucy'. It's not just that Lucy an extremely complete skeleton but the fossils were in excellent state. This means that Lucy gave us a huge quantity of information that is scientifically important concerning our ancestors' earliest ancestors.

A The reconstruction A. Afarensis Skull. Take note of the small Canines and the very small The Cranial Size in comparison to the Eye sockets and the Face.

The skull reconstruction from A. Afarensis, being gazed at By Donald Johanson. Notice that the smaller size of the brain is a reflection of a smaller overall size.

Like other Australopithecus graciles, A. afarensis had canines and molars that were small for an ape, yet large enough for modern humans, having a brain and body that were the size of the modern chimpanzee as well as the ability to climb trees effortlessly. A. Afarensis's big toe however had gone from grasping to being straight and shorter which was better suited for bipedal walking. This species was also improving its walking. Computer simulations indicate that A. Afarensis had a a gate that was similar to humans today, but not as sophisticated. In addition, infants couldn't more hold on to the fur of their mothers as infants of the great apes as their large toe was no longer able to grasp. This suggests A. Afarensis was not able to spend a lot of time climbing trees and needed their hands to support and clasp their babies.

Casts of the Fossils Remains of "Lucy," a well known A. Afarensis. Left image shows an 3D Positioning, and the right image shows the Fossils laid flat. It is important to note it's a long way from a Complete Skeleton Although it's an Excellent Example of Fossils of this Age.

Two reconstructions of Lucy. On the left, you can see an entire Skeletal Reconstruction. It is evident that the Brown Bones are Casts of the actual fossils, while the white 'Bones' are plastic sections created by extrapolation using Symmetry as well as other A. Afarensis Fossil Finds. Notice that the Long Arms with Deeply Curved fingers that are suited to climbing, but a wide, forward the femur is oriented and flat Feet Well Suited to Walking. On the right is a suggestion of what Lucy might have looked like In Her Life, Complete with Fur and Skin.

Next, the gracile Australopithecus species, A. africanus (note that A. africanus is different from A. afarensis) is depicted by fossils dating between 3.3 million years up to 2.1 million years. A. africanus appears to be a descendant of A. A. afarensis. Since the timelines of their existences are overlapping, it suggests the possibility that A. Africanus evolved from an isolated population of A. A. afarensis. The most well-known A. africanus fossil, discovered in the hands of Raymond Dart in South Africa is known as the "Taung Child'. It was a fairly full skull from a young person and the Foramen Magnum clearly located at the bottom of the skull. The skull is unique because a large portion of the bones on the back of the skull were broken off probably shortly after death. A clear image of the brain fossil can be seen.

Taung Child Fossil containing Fossilized Imprints of Brain

The 1920's saw the discovery of in the 1920's, Taung Child was a significant eye opener in the 1920's. It provided the first convincing evidence of a distinct species between humans and apes. Since that first discovery, numerous fossils of A. africanus have been discovered. Together , these fossils proved that bipedalism was developed prior to the development of an expanded brain. This came as a shock to numerous scientists of the day who believed that intelligence was a requirement for walking. A. africanus is similar to A. Afarensis and preserved the fingers that were extremely curled and arms that were long. Other features found in fossils of feet and legs but suggest improvements to the gait of walking.

Australopithecus garhi was one of the last gracile Australopithecus species that been around between 2 and 3 million years between 3 and 2 million years ago. It is believed that they originated out of A. africanus as an off-branch of A. africanus. First fossils from A. Garhi were discovered in Ethiopia in the year 1996. Although its brain size is not as large as that of other gracile Australopithecus species, A. garhi appears to possess some characteristics in the fossils of the leg and arm bones which are much more advanced than A. Afarensis or A. africanus.

Construction of Skull of A. garhi. The blue Sections are missing Skull Sections.

Australopithecus Sediba is also an eminent species of gracile Australopithecus with fossils from six individuals discovered within South Africa in 2008. The fossils are bones that have been broken and a comparatively fully intact and complete skull. They were found to be around two million years of age. The fossils look like A. Afarensis, however, fingers are more dexterous. While A. farensis was characterized by large curled hands, A. sediba had smaller fingers that did not have the curly. The resultant grip and opposable thumb are more typical for humans and not apes. They are better suited to use tools rather than climbing trees.

The skull of A. sediba

forearms and hands of A. S. sediba (left) and The Hands of A. Sediba in the palm of a Modern Person (right).

It is believed that A. sediba and its apparent resemblances to A. Afarensis were awe-inspiring to many paleoanthropologists because A. A. afarensis has disappeared from fossil records 2.9 million years old, or nearly one million years prior to the appearance of A. sediba. This suggests a resemblance of A. A. afarensis that extends beyond the fossil record discovered, or an earlier emergence of A. Sediba, which is more likely than the fossil record we have suggests. It is possible that future fossils will shed light on the connection with A. sediba and A. A. afarensis.

After having reviewed the Australopithecus gracile species and then turning towards the more powerful species. Like we said, they were larger than the gracile species having large skulls, massive jaws as well as large mashing molars. While they appeared to be more powerful however, they lived on a diet that was primarily composed of fibrous plant matter, fruits as well as seeds, nuts and. If the gracile Australopithecus are like Chimpanzees, the robust Australopithecus is similar to gorillaswho are also fed mostly composed of soft plant matter such as nuts, grubs and nuts. The teeth fossilized by Australopithecus's robust species are found to be flat, indicating the fact that they eat a tough, fibrous diet.

The first fossils of these strong Australopithecus species date back the beginning of 2.7 million years old. The oldest fossils date from 1.1

million years old. The Australopithecus robust originated from the earlier Australopithecus gracile which is most likely A. africanus. Since there is a similarity between the chronology of A. africanus with the robust species, it is believed that some pockets in A. africanus became isolated in areas of remoteness which provided very hard sources of food. This resulted in the evolution into the more robust species which had very large and robust jaws that were powered by massive muscles. The jaw bone of the gorilla was attached to the skull's top through a bony ridge, referred to as a'sagittal-cranial"crest"' that is similar to the one that the modern gorilla.

A. boisei's Skull A. boisei showing distinct Sagittal Cranial Crest running along the Skull as well as the massive lower Jaw as well as Teeth. This Fossil was nicknamed "Nutcracker Man" because of obvious reasons.

The skeletons of no Australopithecus robust species have been discovered and the fossils we have are small. However, from these fossils we can infer that Australopithecus robust preserved the small brains of the gracile species. Also, they were slightly larger and more heavily muscular. The males averaged between 4 feet 3 inches and 4 feet seven inches (1.3 to 1.4 meters) in height, and females much smaller. Although they retained an inclination to walk like their ancestors the robust gorillas are believed to have retreated to forests that were heavily forested that are like the ones those where modern gorillas are found. It was only in such a setting that their food source of leaves and other tough vegetation could be seen.

The species comprising the three tough Australopithecus comprise A. Aethiopicus A. boisei and A. robustus. Of these, Australopithecus A. aethiopicus is believed to be the one to evolve fossils that date as long as 2.7 millions of years. First fossils from A. Aethiopicus were discovered in Ethiopia in the year 1967. The infamous 'Black Skull' was discovered at Kenya in 1985. Manganese found in the ground that surrounds the fossil had turned the fossilized bone into an opaque black sheen. It is believed the possibility that A. boisei as well as A. robustus derived from A. A. aethiopicus. A. Aethiopicus was akin to other species of robust however it had more archaic characteristics such as higher cheek bones as well as an extended jaw line which pushed the lower jaw forward. The distinctive shape on the facial features strongly suggest that tough Australopithecus diverged from the ancestral line of humans.

Fossil of the famous "Black Skull of A. Aethiopicus

Primarily discovered in Tanzania The oldest fossils of Australopithecus were discovered 2.4 millennia ago. Meanwhile, the oldest fossils discovered date back 1.4 million years ago. As with other Australopithecus that were robust, the brain body that was A. boisei is tiny while the teeth appeared huge and their molars were four times larger than modern humans, and covering more than twice its surface. With an sagittal crest that was distinctive, "Nutcracker Man" had jaws that were extremely powerful and suited to crush tough vegetative matter. The huge jaw and teeth of A. boisei provided what been perceived as an enormously large face.

The skull's shape between the fossils from A. boisei suggest that this was a dispersed species, which was undergoing an array of adaptive strategies to live. A. boisei is more massive than A. Aethiopicus, and was continuing on the path towards becoming more like a gorilla. There was also a distinct amount in sexual dimorphism (variation in the size of males and females) and males weighing an average of 100 pounds (49 kg) and measuring four feet six inches tall (1.37 meters) and females weighing approximately 75 pounds (34 kg) and stood at around 4 feet 1 inch (1.24 metres).

Skull from A. boisei and suggestions for reconstruction.

The entire species of Australopithecus both robust and gracile alike, displayed the same degree of sexual dimorphism, similar to the one shown in A. boisei, which is in between modern chimpanzees and humans. The amount of sexual dimorphism between animals, which is similar to the size of the canine teeth can be a sign of the amount of male competition with females. The greater the level of sexual dimorphism as well as the bigger the canine teeth, generally the greater the number of females associated with the most dominant males. For instance, the more powerful male lions and chimpanzees usually have the privilege of mating with half a dozen or more females. The species with a low level of sexual dimorphism are more likely to mat with one male, and male. In humans of today, this difference is on the region of just 15 percent (i.e. that a male of modern times is just 15% bigger than a female of the same age). For chimpanzees, this value is around 50 percent. Australopithecus species were in with chimps and us consequently, it is believed that they could have formed families with females grouped with males who were stronger.

The final of the tough species Australopithecus robustus is only observed within South Africa.

A. robustus has jaws with more advanced specialized than its cousins from north which is likely due to the foods that are available. The analysis suggests that, while A. Aethiopicus as well as A. boisei primarily ate hard foods like leaves A. robustus could have thrived on hard food sources like nuts, seeds and tubers. The fossils found in A. robustus are from between two million to 1.2 million years old, which makes it the final species of species in the Australopithecus group of species that grow. A. robustus was not much taller than A. boisei however they were a little heavier. Evidence suggests that males were about 4 feet tall (1.2 meters) and weighed about 120 pounds (54 kg) while females were around three feet and two inches tall (1 meters) and weighed around 90 pounds (40 kg). Thus, the species was following its evolution towards an animal-like species but was far from the route that was to eventually lead to humankind.

The Fossil Reconstructed Skull from A. robustus.

In the end, Australopithecus was a very efficient evolutionary line. With Australopithecus Anamensis appearing on the stage as long as 4.4 million years ago, and Australopithecus robustus only leaving the stage about 1.2 million years old, this bipedal genus of land-based hominins strolled the Earth for over three million years. However, following 1.2 million years, the fossil record does not contain evidence for Australopithecus. The genus has gone extinct. There is speculation that these species were extinct because of being unable to continue to adjust to the ever changing environment. It is more likely that the entire lineage of Australopithecus flinched under the pressures of competition imposed on them by a different species of hominin. The genus had ironically developed from Australopithecus. The genus is called Homo which means 'man'. It is the very first species belonging to this new genus we pay attention.

Chapter 6: Our African Origins - Homo Habilis

The first species that was identified in the Genus Homo and, consequently, acknowledged by the same species that we are was named Homo Habilis. H. Habilis was a mysterious hominin leaving behind a very solitary fossil document about its presence. It is believed that the species first appeared somewhere between 2.5 millions of years ago and then went extinct 1.5 million years in the past. This implies that H. is actually coexists with the majority other Australopithecus species and went extinct before the last of the species that was robust of Australopithecus.

Based on the very limited fossil evidence, H. habilis appears in a variety of aspects to have a physiological related to the Australopithecus species with gracile gracile. Actually, due to the limited fossils related to H. Habilis, and the similarities of the fossils found to Australopithecus There were a number of debates about whether the fossils were part of an exclusive genus, just another species of

Australopithecus or were an amalgamation of several previously known Australopithecus species. There is a consensus that H. Habilis is a distinct species, and was the first one to merit the designation of genus Homo.

It was first thought that H. was habilis arose from A. Sediba, which was the final and most advanced of the Australopithecus graciles. There are two issues with this assertion however. The first is that certain among the oldest H. fossils from habilis seem to predate the appearance of A. Sediba. Additionally, these older H. Habilis fossils seem to be lacking in the level of physiological sophistication in comparison to A. Sediba. However, they are conserving the curved fingers and shorter legs of the more primitive Australopithecus. This is why it's been proposed that H. Habilis evolved out of either A. Afarensis and A. africanus. Given the lack of H. theabilis evidence it is impossible to be certain what Australopithecus was the ancestral species of the first Homo species.

H. Habilis was roughly similar in size to Australopithecus graciles in general with a height of 5 feet and 3 inches (1.3 meters) in average. Furthermore, H. Habilis was small in canines, but large molars that were that were similar to Australopithecus. The analysis of the microwear texture of teeth, conducted by looking at the patterns of wear on tooth fossils under microscope suggests that H. Habilis was an omnivore as was the gracious Australopithecus that ate a mixture of soft plants as well as meat. However, in other ways, H. habilis was distinct from Australopithecus. H. Habilis was also distinguished by features the transition to a more human physiological physiology, which earned its place in the Homo genus. Homo.

While the earliest H. Habilis fossils seemed to have very short legs Later fossils (i.e. older) have legs that are significantly longer than the other Australopithecus species. The oldest fossils from H. H. habilis were equipped with hands that were designed for climbing tree branches, the hands grew more refined to manipulate older fossils, far exceeding the strength in any of the Australopithecus species. This suggests that as H. the evolution of H. habilis moved away from Australopithecus it developed more human-like traits.

H. Habilis also featured a face considerably smaller than Australopithecus and gave it an appearance more human than the ape-like look of Australopithecus. The protrusion of an animal's face, for example, the snouts of dogs, helps it bite. The smaller canines and the flattened face suggest that H. Habilis didn't combat with its teeth, not even when they were fighting. A more flatter face, however, is required to enhance vocalization capabilities. H. Habilis also had an encasement for the brain that was more extensive than Australopithecus. In contrast to the gracile and robust species that were part of Australopithecus had brains around 1/3 the size of modern human brain, H. habilis possessed an average of half the size of us.

The brain of all animals is constantly working and requires more energy than other organs in the body. So, the brain of an animal will only begin to larger size when this expansion results in a benefit when it comes to getting more food. This is necessary to offset the higher power consumption of the larger brain. This is the reason why herding animals don't seem very bright. You can take as much grass as you like with a tiny brain. They gain more from changing their running style to speed up instead of becoming more intelligent. Predators, however, are more sophisticated, since they use their brains to find their prey however, becoming ever more intelligent will not provide them with more food. Usually, getting larger teeth or claws that are longer is more efficient. The method used by animals to increase its survival rate by expanding their brain size is not common in evolutionary evolution and is usually only seen when there are no other viable ways to go.

The brains of H. Habilis increased its capacity to capture food and likely its general capacity to reproduce and survive. It is believed that H. Habilis could have achieved these feats by using its bigger brain to enhance social cooperation. Vocalizations are crucial to successful social interaction. However, this isn't to suggest it was the case that H. habilis spoke. The language is far from being a common language from hominids. But the sophistication of tones and the implied emotional state in the sound produced from the device that produces voice sounds of H. Habilis could be sufficient to result in greater social understanding. Better cooperation among members of the collection of H. H. habilis while collecting food as well as protecting their young and in defending themselves against predators could have increased their survival as an entire species. The whole thing is simply a theory based on educated speculation and is not able to be definitively proven using the very limited fossil evidence, but the theory is plausible enough.

The Skull Homo Habilis and Artistic Reconstruction of their Possible Appearance

What else can H. Habilis be able to do using this new mental capacity? In addition, crucial to their accomplishment, H. Habilis was able successfully to utilize stone tools. Although basic stone tools were discovered in conjunction and Australopithecus fossils, the evidence is overwhelming that H. Habilis was a frequent user in the use of stones. They were, in reality, deliberately made by H. H. habilis in order to meet certain specifications. "Habilis" means "handy" in Latin and , therefore, Homo habilis is the 'Handy Man'. The name was given to the species due to the extensive collection of stone tools that were discovered with H. the fossils of habilis. Their brains are larger and therefore gave H. Habilis with the capability to design and develop tools capable of be used for collecting food and food processing as well as to defend itself against predators.

Stones that are clearly tools have been discovered in H. Habilis as long to 2.5 millennia old, at the time of its emergence. These tools were higher-quality than those discovered in Australopithecus. They were made up of stones with natural geometries that were well-suited to different tasks like cutting meat, breaking open bones and scraping skins. As H. Habilis continued to advance it was also evolving in terms of manual dexterity, and possibly in terms of intelligence more advanced stones were discovered alongside fossils. This clearly involved the intentional shaping of the stones, by hitting them together to create pieces. This method can generate specific geometries for tools specifically with regard to creating sharp edges that are that are suitable to cut.

Later, H. habilis was able to create what is now known as the "Lower Paleolithic Oldowan Tool Set'. These were stone tools that had flaked edges with a variety of shapes employed for cutting meat to take meat from bones and in order to skin animal skins, break bones of animals, open nuts, and prepare food items made of plants. Bones from large game animals with distinctive cuts on them or have been cracked open have been discovered as a result of the stone tools that created these marks, employed in the process of cutting meat away or gaining access to bone marrow.

View from the Front View (left) as well as Side View (right) of typical Olduwan Scrapers of the Lower Paleolithic. Although they are not sophisticated tools However, they provide a major advantage over Stones that naturally occur.

Although many of these instruments were designed specifically for the preparation of meat, none of them have been associated with hunting. H. Habilis may have been able to capture snakes, rabbits or slugs. and then consume them. The stones were designed to be used for processing larger game, which H. Habilis is not believed to kill. So it is believed that H. Habilis was likely to have been a scavenger for big game. Much like modern-day hyenas H. Habilis may have let predators with large size such as lions perform the actual hunting. Then, they orally snatched these predators away from their quarry or ate the remains after predators had consumed their food. The predatory animal likely consumed the majority of the carcass and hyenas had already broken smaller bones with their jaws of strength, H. habilis might be left with just the biggest bones. By smashing them using a stone tool, they were able to access the fatty tissues that are high in calories inside.

The tools developed by H. Habilis were not suitable for defense against prey or attacks by others from its own species. Australopithecus. It is possible that they hurled rocks at predators to scare them away or waved branches at them as do modern Chimpanzees. In the case of other hominins, they might not utilize tools when fighting occurred between groups or utilized a tool of chance like taking a rock to strike their adversaries with. However, H. habilis did not develop tools specifically for attack. This suggests that H. H. habilis may not have been an especially dangerous species.

The Carta of Africa Showing Places where Oldowan Tools have been found

Stone palm-sized choppers which are that are representative of the Oldowan tool-making culture date back to around two million years old. While they are typically located within East Africa, where H. Habilis is believed to evolve but these choppers have been discovered in other areas in Africa and beyond and as far south as the present day South Africa to as far north as the High Plateaus in Algeria. Thus, H. Habilis was adaptable and adaptable enough to leave the environment that was favorable to them in which it developed and to expand across a wide range of geographical environments.

As Australopithecus, H. habilis was quite small, slow and ineffective and had no speed to escape an animal predator, nor big teeth and claws to defend themselves. This makes them extremely susceptible to attacks. In contrast to Australopithecus which could scurry through nearby trees to avoid prey, H. Habilis wasn't not a shrewd climber. So they had another way to defend themselves. It is believed that they utilized their higher intelligence to organize themselves and cooperate in tackling threats. For instance, when an lion was approaching one of the males, they could have been able to approach the lion in a group and hurled stones at it to frighten away.

Let's look at for a moment the nature of the brain as well as the basis of intelligence. The brain is comprised of "neurons", the cells that make up our nervous system as well as the the brain of all mammals. The majority of neurons that make up the brain serve to control various organs, muscles, and nerve impulses of animals. For instance, an elephant has a brain that is massive because it has a huge body. This is why we talk about the size of the brain in relation to the dimension of the elephant. This is also known as "encephalization". A larger brain in comparison in size leads to the availability of more neurons for thinking in addition to controlling our breathing and digestion. The neurons that are thought to be thinking tend to be concentrated along the surface of a thin layer, typically less than one millimeter thick (1/8th of an inch) which is found on the outside of our brain. Therefore, a larger brain will provide a greater surface area for the brain, and thus more neurons available to think about.

There is more to mental capability beyond the size of the brain. There are various ways to increase the size of the brain and thus enhance the quantity of brain neurons. This is by introducing folding to the brain's surface. If you've ever looked at images of birds' brain, you may remember that the surface is smooth. If you can recall humans' brains, it's very complicated. These convolutions significantly increase the surface area of the brain, which increases the number of neurons in the brain's thin layer. brain that participate actively thinking. While it's difficult to confirm, it is thought that H. Habilis may have experienced more folding in its brain than Australopithecus. This could have given H. H. habilis an even greater amount of intelligence that was higher in comparison to Australopithecus than their comparative brain size might suggest.

Comparative Analysis of Brain Folds and the Size of the Brain Comparative to Size of Animals (Estimated) in Rat, Cat, Chimpanzee and Human. Human Brains are not only larger in comparison to our body Size However, the Convolutions are Additionally more extensive. This is the reason why Chimps can also be quite intelligent.

Another important factor that affects intelligence is the amount of the 'dendrites' inside the brain. They connect neurons. Every neuron is equipped with a set of branches or dendrites that extend from it. They allow 'communication' with other neurons via the exchange of "neural transmitters that are located between dendrites. It is the capability of neurons to talk to themselves that gives them the capability to control the body and gives people the capability to "think'. The higher the number of other neurons each neuron is able to communicate with, the more intelligence of the neuron will be. Thus, 'neural dendritic dense is an important factor in intelligence.

A magnified image of an Neuron (center) as well as Dendrites in the brain. Neurons are the same in all Animals. Human Neurons are exactly the same as Worm Neurons. We just have a lot of neurons. And very long dendrites that connect them.

Dendrite density is controlled by the length average of every dendrite. Dendrites that are short only allow each neuron to talk to just a few of its neighbours. Dendrites that are longer allow for more neuron-to-neuron interaction.

The paleoanthropologists believe that H. Habilis had a greater Dendritic densities than Australopithecus. Australopithecus is also believed to have had a greater dendritic density over its contemporaries. The reason for this is numerous genetic studies that have discovered at least one gene that determine how long dendrites are. The gene is named SRGAP2. SRGAP2 is a unique gene in particular, particularly when you're a human.

The gene SRGAP2 is found throughout all species. However , in humans SRGAP2 has been duplicated several times, leading to humans having dendrites much longer than other species. As an example, the typical neural dendrite in a dog is on the range of 25 millimeters (one one inch) long. For humans, however, dendrites of our brains can reach 1000 millimeters (over three inches) long. Humans have a lot more processing power than other species for each neuron involved in cognition. The processing capacity of the brain is increased by 10 times as different species of animals develop like reptiles from fish, amphibians from amphibians, and mammals from reptiles. However, humans possess 100 times the processing power of the typical mammal. Humans also have a level of brain growth that is usually connected with two phases of evolution. This is an incredibly shocking real. What is the reason that the brains of our ancestors' ancestors' have grown at such a rate and in such a short time? Also what is the reason?

The first question is question of how. Humans have what is known as a duplicate SRGAP2 gene. The way we evolved is that along our evolutionary line, duplication mistakes were discovered on the gene material that is associated with SRGAP2. Genetic defects are prevalent in all living things like animals, plants and bacterial, when they reproduce. When cells undergo division, certain DNA segments may be misplaced or duplicated. These genetic mistakes are generally not preserved within a species. The most common variant of the gene is likely to be dominant. However, sometimes, these mistakes can be advantageous for the species. In these instances, the 'errors' are actually enhancements. The new genes are more likely be kept since it improves the survival and fertility percentage of people with it.

In humans SRGAP2 is a human gene. SRGAP2 was duplicated not just one time however, but three times with each one of the replications being stored in the common gene pool. The result was to dramatically extend the size of dendrites of our brains and, consequently our ability to think. Genetic researchers have discovered through regression techniques that duplications first took place approximately 3.4 millennia ago. This is in line to an appearance Australopithecus. Another duplication took place around 2.4 millions of years later. It is important to note that this coincides to the time of the introduction of H. Habilis. A further duplication was also observed approximately one million years back. This is in line to the appearance of another hominin about which we'll speak about in the near future.

The duplication of this gene can be only seen in humans. If gene replication are widespread in all animals, and if all animals carry the SRGAP2 gene it is likely that other animals were also affected by duplicates of this gene through the millennia of evolution. Why do we only observe the duplicate in humans? Actually, it is preserved several times. This is a reference to the assertion that hominins, when they were forced to be as a barefooted creature and walk with two feet were very vulnerable to attack by predators , and were unable to access food sources. We could not run away, and we couldn't hide , and we were unable to effectively defend ourselves. There weren't any trees to harvest fruit from. To be alive, our sole chance of survival was growing smarter and more quickly. In the case of other animals that randomly stumbled to duplicate SRGAP2 genes, the duplication was unnoticed by other animals. SRGAP2 gene, it was largely unnoticed. A deer with a slightly higher intelligence level doesn't have a better chance of survival, therefore, duplication of this gene will not always mean that it is preferentially kept. For early hominins however, being smarter provided a significant benefit. The people who have the duplicated gene were likely to live long and produce strong children. For those who were born without duplication they were more likely to be eaten.

Imagine that a woman is carrying the duplication SRGAP2 gene, while the man she has children with doesn't. Are the children born with the gene? Yes, but others won't. The ones with the gene be more likely to live and have children more effectively than those without. Therefore, genes with strong characteristics tend to grow in frequency as time passes, with many generations preserving and further promoting the gene. The weaker genes are in however eventually eliminated. This is true for other beneficial genes too We will learn more about this in the future.

While the skull and brain dimensions of H. Habilis may not have been much bigger than Australopithecus however, they were significantly more intelligent. While they provided the evolutionary advantages to a fragile and vulnerable species the price of adding knowledge to H. H. habilis was significant. The more sophisticated it is in its brain, higher power that is required to run that brain. A brain that is smart consumes a significant amount of calories. So, to allow H. Habilis to be able to live the harsh environment, their more advanced brain has to have given them the ability to beat their foes and consume greater quantities of food. It is believed that this was accomplished by raising the social complexity in the species. For instance, some people may have been focused on gathering food to feed the community, while others concentrated on protecting the children. Of course, we'll never determine with certainty whether H. Habilis utilized their higher brain power in their favor, however the speculations are plausible.

As previously mentioned, H. habilis evolved approximately 2.4 millennia ago. It was extinct 1.5 million years later. This is roughly when the other Australopithecus species became extinct. The reasons for the extinction of species are numerous. The species could go extinct due to its inability to adapt to the changing the environment and climate. In other cases, a part of a species could develop into a new species that exceeds the previous species, and causes it to go into the brink of extinction. As you might guess, an entirely new, stronger, more efficient and more sophisticated species emerged from H. Habilis. This new species likely has driven H. Habilis and the Australopithecus remnants to the brink of extinction.

The Asian Adventurer - Homo erectus

Homo habilis lived on earth for about one millions of years. That isn't an awful amount of time for a species. Their demise was not due to any flaw by them and was more due to their remarkable achievement as an animal species. H. Habilis mutated and changed into a new species, but it was far more advanced and efficient than the ones they. This new species is often referred to as Homo erectus. H. Erectus is believed to have evolved around 1.9 millennia ago. H. is erectus and H. the habilis species is likely to be observed that they co-existed for about 400 000 years. H. fossils of H. erectus have been discovered across Tanzania, Ethiopia, Kenya and South Africa. They are also the very first hominins to be who were able to colonize the world beyond Africa. The remains of their remains were discovered in Europe as well as in clear throughout all over the Asian continent. The oldest fossils of H. Erectus date back to only four50,000 years old.

The magnitude of the physical change between H. Habilis and H. the erectus is substantial. H. was erectus had a more straight spine and shorter toes as compared to H. Habilis, and thus was a better walker. Hands were more sophisticated and better at manipulating tools and objects as compared to the hands of H. H. habilis, who retained the tree climbing characteristics. H. erectus possessed arms that were of the same proportions to the human body as modern humans, in contrast, H. Habilis kept the long, tree-climbing arms of Australopithecus. Also, the shoulder of H. Erectus were quite similar to contemporary humans. This suggests they could throw objects in the same way that we can. H. Erectus could therefore be able to use tools that could projectile for the purpose of hunting or for defense.

The main distinction that distinguished H. Habilis and H. erectus was in their proportions to their bodies. While H. habilis was diminutive and had a barrel chest similar to an ape, H. Erectus was tall and slim, with males on average five feet and 10 inches (1.77 metres) at the height. It was as tall as modern-day men from countries where nutrition levels are high and more than the global average size for modern men. Females were about 80percent larger than males. This means that H. Erectus showed smaller sexual dimorphism than H. the habilis. This indicates that the development of nuclear families that was based on the union of one man and one woman was already in full swing. The advantages of this type of family uniting increased the likelihood of survival and children received more care and security from their fathers, as well as their mothers.

Nearly Complete Skeleton of Homo Erectus (left) discovered at the time of 1984 Richard Leakey and Dated to 1.6 million years old. Also known as the 'Turkana Boys' The Skeleton is of a boy who is estimated to be between 7 and 11 years old. The woman on the right is a Paleoanthropologist, who is part of Leakey's Team that Lays alongside Turkana Boy. The Skeleton is surprisingly modern in many ways.

A Comparative Analysis between the adult Skeleton of Homo Erectus versus The Australopithecus afarensis Fossil Lucy, who was just 3'7" (1.1 metres). Lucy can be seen as a Walking Chimpanzee. H. Erectus through Contrast is a lot more apparent as an Human.

The skulls of H. Erectus also differed in a significant way from that of H. H. First, H. erectus had an incredibly larger brain than H. H. This was in part a result of H. Erectus being bigger. There is also an increase in the size of the brain too. This resulted in a bigger with a more balanced skull however, it would be considered flat by contemporary standards. The brow ridge is nonetheless substantial, however it was drastically reduced when compared to H. Habilis. The mandible, or jaw of H. Erectus was thin when compared to H. Habilis, and the premolars, molars, and molars as well as being significantly smaller. This indicates that H. Erectus had not consumed plants that were tough as the predecessors. Teeth wear analysis proves that H. is an omnivore that ate the same broad variety of food. While the teeth in the back of H. the erectus were shorter than those of H. Habilis but their teeth were larger than the modern human.

A Reconstructed Skull from a Homo Erectus adult (top) shows the Human Looking Face, but with large teeth and a smaller Skull Cap as shown. Below is a comparison of the Modern Human Skull Versus a H. Erectus Skull. Notice that the Long Flat Shape to the back of the Skull, the receding Chin along with The Heavy Brow Ridge, Indicated by the Arrow.

With these characteristics, in the end the face of H. Erectus was more human-like than the faces of H. H. habilis or Australopithecus. When we view the reconstruction of the facial features of H. Habilis, based on fossilized skulls, our initial impression is that of an ape's face. If we stare at the face in the fashion of H. Erectus we get the distinct impression that have for the first time gazing at the face of a human. A person who isn't attractive to be sure, but by any means However, their advancement towards humankind is evident.

It is also thought to be the case that H. erectus probably had less body hair than H. the habilis, or Australopithecus and Australopithecus, which also have less body hair than the modern Apes. The loss of hair is attributed to the fact that we've moved onto open Savannah. Being constantly in warm and open landscape causes the production of heat in our bodies. This heat requires to be shed. This is accomplished through the increase in the density of sweat glands that line our skin. The sweat glands of humans are 10 times higher than that of primate. The loss of hair on our bodies was essential to allow the sweat glands to fulfill their function effectively. It is believed that hair was left on our head to shield the skin from the glare of direct sunlight.

There are additional benefits that the reduction in body hair could also bring. It is possible that the ability to reveal facial features helped early hominins communicate their emotions more clearly as well as improving their the way they communicated with their emotions. A majority of apes do not have facial hair, which is believed to be the reason. Additionally, the prevalence that lice, and parasites are present will be reduced, which would reduce the risk of diseases. A fascinating study on lice found how the head louse found in humans is quite like the body louse of the chimps. It is believed that this change was made approximately three millennia ago. It is therefore reasonable to assume that this was the time when hominins shed their heavy body hair.

First fossils from H. Erectus were discovered in the Indonesian island Java that is now part of modern day Indonesia in 1891. The fossils were a mystery to the person who discovered them and the discovery was known as "Java Man". The fossils discovered later in China and later referred to as "Peking Man" were identified as being similar in appearance to Java Man. The two discoveries were later recognized as being of the same species, and was named Homo erectus. "Erectus" is a reference to "upright" which is why Homo erectus means "upright man" reflecting their massive and powerful size. Since then, there have been more than 200 fossils that represent over 40 people have been discovered of H. Erectus.

Homo erectus is found to have spread across Africa and into Europe and along the South East Asian Coastline, including the Far South as the Island of Java in Modern Day Indonesia.

Due to the vast area that H. Erectus was found and the extended period of time during which H. developed various localized variations are believed to be present in the fossil records of H. Erectus. This is why H. the erectus is usually classified into'sub-species'. For example, the sub-species of H. the erectus who remained in Africa are usually known as Homo Erectus ergaster or, more simply, as Homo Ergaster. The ones that moved to Asia are often called

Homo sensu stricto erectus. There are other names that have been proposed for different populations, but we'll stick to the common Homo Erectus since, regardless of the distances and decades, they appears to remain one breeding population.

The findings of H. Erectus fossils from Africa are quite scarce. The reason behind this is unclear. They are more common all over Asia and it's because of this that early paleoanthropologists believed that humankind was born in Asia instead of Africa. In the context of reasons we'll explore in the future, it is recognized to not be the situation. In any case, the dearth of specimens of H. the erectus found in Africa is a unique feature. The few specimens that have been discovered were found in the eastern and southern regions of Africa The most recent dating from 1.4 million years old.

For H. Erectus in Asia The majority of paleoanthropologists think based on the archaeological evidence suggesting that H. was erectus came to the region from Africa frequently throughout their history. Because there was no map, the populations moved in the direction of the food sources, and often wandered across the continent. Newcomers to Asia likely bred with people who were already there, thereby creating their own DNA. In the Asian weather can prove quite brutal and has been known to fluctuate greatly over long durations of time, ranging between warmer and wetter to dry and cold. The Asian colonists may have suffered extremely when the weather turned against them as it's believed H. Erectus populations across Asia declined significantly, and then retreated to the south when it became cold. So H. population of erectus in Asia may have been destroyed during cold and drought episodes and then replenished and renewed by fresh arrivals of Africa as the moisture and warmth returned.

The first time it evolved as a distinct species around 1.9 millennia ago H. I. erectus continued develop and evolve throughout their existence through the following one and a half million years or as. The fossils of individuals dating back to 1.9 million years back were not physically sophisticated as those that were discovered only 450,000 years ago. The earliest H. populations of erectus tend to have archaic features, more similar to H. the habilis species, and are shorter and having less developed faces. The tall, well-built human-like H. fossils of erectus discovered later reflect the evolution of a million years of improvement. The brain casing was discovered to grow in size as the passage of time. When African H. Erectus and earlier migratory groups of H. Erectus from Asia had skulls ranging from 700 to 900 cm3 in size Later fossils were found to be ranging from 900 to 1100 cm3. While the earlier value was approximately 55% of the size of modern humans and the latter is closer to 70%..

The increased mental capacity of the brain assisted H. erectus in achieving significant advancements in tools making compared to H. Habilis. Ergaster is Greek for "workman" and was chosen to refer to people from the African communities of H. Erectus due to the advanced stone tools typically found in conjunction with African H. the fossils of H. erectus. The skills they use to make tools are known as the Acheulean tool-making industry. This technique of making tools was first introduced about 1.75 million years ago when it was H. Erectus, and continued to be used with a variety of human populations about 130,000 years ago.

While H. Habilis created the relatively basic tools typical in Oldowan technologies, H. erectus was capable of creating bifacial-axe blades as well as massive cleavers. The blades indicate active processing and hunting of massive prey. It is believed that H. the erectus could hunt in groups that were coordinated, a sign of higher levels of socialization. With bigger bodies and bigger brains in relation to body size compared to hominins from earlier times, H. erectus clearly required a lot more calories. It is therefore believed that the species at the least enriched in scavenging and hunting. It is possible they could have developed into adept active hunters, however concrete evidence isn't available.

It is believed that the Oldowan equipment of H. Habilis as well as of the very early H. Erectus were built by striking a stone using an Hammerstone (large stone that was chosen to be struck by another). The flake that comes off from the stone has an innately sharp edge, perfect for cutting and scraping. The core (the stone from which the flake were taken from) can also be used to chop tools, but it was generally removed. Acheulean tools, however, focused on the production of a well-controlled core, with the flakes being either discarded or transformed into smaller tools by bending to create new cores. As the industry developed, the Acheulean manufacturing industry, stone cores were slowly and carefully crafted by experts to create precisely shaped, symmetric and efficient tools.

A few examples that show Examples of Bifacial Hand Axes. Notice that the Material has been selectively Removed from two Edges and both Sides of the Stone to make the Relatively smooth and sharp Double Edge. They could have been used for Butchering Meat but they could have also been employed to go on hunts with The Grooves that are suitable to be used as a handle are evident.

In order to create these symmetric tools, the hammerstone was used first to roughen the shape of the stone, by slowly stripping away the material around the core. The resulting core was thinned by taking smaller and finer flakes with an elongated and smaller Hammer, like the bone, or antler. To make sure that the hammerstone did not slide when struck, the stone's surface was removed using a different stone. The final shaping process was made to ensure a perfect cutting edge, and a snug fitting in the palm of the hand. The outcome of Acheulean tool manufacturing was not just an improved tool with sharper edges over the one that Oldowan methods of making tools however, it also had a longer cutting edge. It was averaging 8.8 inches (20 cm) as opposed to just 2 inches (5 centimeters) for Oldowan tools.

While fewer fossils from H. Erectus were found in Africa in comparison to Asia and the opposite is the case with stones found in stone tools. Many more Acheulean type stones have been discovered throughout Africa than Asia as well as the of distribution decreasing as one moves farther away from Africa. It is evident that the distribution pattern in Acheulean stone tools actually gives more information than fossil finds from the areas where H. extinctus lived and their respective populations. Preservation of fossils is heavily dependent on the environmental conditions. However, it is true that stone tools are preserved in the archaeological record irrespective of the environmental conditions. The widespread distribution of stone tools indicates that the number of H. Erectus in Africa was much greater than those in Asia. The lack of this apparent proportion in the fossil evidence of H. Erectus may be due to the dry climate in Asia being more suited to creating fossils than the humid African climate.

The distribution map of the stone tool above shows the high density of H. Erectus populations, not only in Africa but throughout Europe too, mainly across Spain and France There are fewer instances to England as well as Italy. The concentrations are also very high on the western side of Arabia as well as in India and between the two regions. Despite the numerous discoveries of H. the erectus fossils found in the present day China Stone tool concentrations indicate that the density of H. Erectus was never excessive in this region. It is also worth noting the existence of stones found in Indonesia which have high concentrations in the islands of Java.

The map of distribution of stone tools provides us with a solid clue about the method by which H. Erectus came from Africa. The map above shows the absence of stone tool evidence in Egypt. This is because the region was historically desert, and therefore unsuitable for human settlement. This land route to exit Africa was not available. How then was H. Erectus able escape from Africa? The answer lies in the distribution of the stone tools map. H. Erectus seems to be having left Africa and travelled direct to Spain and the southernmost tip of Arabia across the narrow stretches of water that separated these two regions from Africa. Then they spread over Europe in Europe and Asia from these locations.

What could be the reason for this in the first place, when these routes were closed by open water? To comprehend this, we need to think about how for long time periods our climate on Earth is constantly changing. There are periodic ice ages, separated by periods of dry and hot conditions. In colder times, the ocean levels decrease and let more land. This decreases the distances between land mass. The rather small distances of open water which separate Africa from Spain and the southern part of Arabia would have been diminished even more during these cooler times. While the separations wouldn't be entirely free of water, the opposite land mass could be seen across the water's smaller stretches. The possibility that H. Erectus traveled across these routes is an indication that they could build rafts that could cross smaller lengths of water.

As H. Erectus spread to Europe as well as southern western Asia, India and south east Asia the materials they used to make their stone tools also changed. Acheulean tools created by H. erectus were created using whatever stone was readily available locally and was most suitable for use in tools. The preferred stone was Flint by the people of Western Europe where it was in abundance. Quartzite and basalt were frequently employed in Africa since they were among the hardest rocks available and therefore the most effective at creating and keeping an edge. Shale, sandstone and limestone tools have been found in places where only these stones were found.

The methods used in Acheulean toolmaking also happened in relation to locations. Axes that were found in the eastern regions of Asia such as South Korea, Mongolia and China were more likely to employ the principal stone core for the tool. In contrast, those that were found in Africa as well as Southwest Asia and India tend to be constructed with the huge flakes of the original core. The secondary cores could later undergo further processing. So two distinct tools making techniques are evidently being developed. Techniques for making tools are not just different based on place but also with the course of time. Stone tools that were made prior to the 600000 year mark were more hefty and less symmetrical, whereas after

600,000 they became lighter and more and symmetric. This indicates an ongoing improvement in the sophistication and the refinement of the tool making process.

Although the Acheulean stone toolmaking method was different depending on the location, a large number of the tools discovered at Asian sites along with H. Erectus fossils were created by the more traditional Oldowan method, whereas this is not the scenario in Africa. This indicates that Africa was the main source of H. the erectus's innovation and innovation, as new technology was transferred to Asia with each wave of immigrants. When large groups of H. Erectus left Africa and travelled across Asia they appeared at times to have lost the ability to create the more advanced tools. It could be an effect of environmental factors which reduced the size of the communities for example, a drought could cause a large group traveling together to break up in smaller units. This would result in the loss of expertise within the remaining members.

Fossils found in H. Erectus, along with hominins of other species are typically discovered in conjunction with fossil bones of species they ate. However , with H. Erectus, these bones of animals are typically discovered in a state of charring and are often found alongside pieces of fire-hardened clay. The clays are required to be heated that are higher than 400degC (750degF) in order to form temperatures that are higher than the ones that are produced by natural fires. The oldest evidence dates back around 1.5 million years old, the existence of this hardened clay suggests the use of fire in a controlled manner. Evidence indicates that H. Erectus made use of the flame for cooking their meals, or perhaps being able to generate the flame at will or perhaps only getting it from time to time by natural sources, such as lightning strikes.

There are numerous important advantages of cooking food. First, the parasites and other organisms responsible for causing illness are eliminated. In addition cooking can break down food fibers. This decreases the amount of calories needed to digest food items as well as broadens the selection of food options that can be consumed, and boosts the amount of calories that can be taken in from foods. So, cooking their food and hunter-gatherers, may be the secret to how H. Erectus could provide the much greater quantity of calories required to sustain their brains and large bodies.

There is evidence to suggest that H. Erectus cooked the majority of their meals also stems from their biochemistry. Hominins like H. habilis and Australopithecus kept massive barrel chests, with an rib cage that was flaring and their large abdomens, which are typical of great Apes. The intestines of animals who consume raw plants must be large in order to digest the many fibers that comprise the food source. H. Erectus was lean and tall and similar to modern human. This implies that their intestines had been reduced in size in comparison to primate species, which is the case for us. This is only possible by the process of cooking vegetables and thereby providing the ability for breaking down bulky cellulous and also to increase the amount of meat in their diet.

The cooking of food has allowed the teeth and jaws of H. Erectus to be less of a prominent feature on the face. Due to the tough cells fibers in their pants, chimpanzees can spend up to five hours per day chewing food to help the intestines take down the fibers. In contrast, humans need to chew their food for an average of 1 hour a day. This is due to the fact that our meals are cooked and thus only a small amount of breaking down of meat and plant fibers is needed by our jaws because cooking already has performed this task.

Another indication that H. Erectus was a fire-user extensively was their journey to Asia. As we have discussed, hominins had already lost most of body hair because of their roots in the scorching open sunlight of the African Savannah. But despite this limitation, H. was erectus grew throughout the harsh, cold climate of Asia. It is difficult to imagine as long as they had access to a fire and possibly clothing and probably some sort of constructed shelter. It's not difficult to imagine that this species, adept at constructing advanced Stone tools was adept at using animal skins to protect itself, as well as wood stones and hides to construct an unassuming hut for living in.

Then we have to ask what kind of life would H. Erectus lived? Paleoanthropologists think that H. was probably in groups that were part of an extended family, just as did the predecessors of their species. This is the way that primates live, as humans until quite recent times. These bands were likely to have travelled with each other, providing protection and care for one another. Although there isn't any solid evidence for this but it is accepted that H. Erectus existed as a hunter-gather society. Males would have hunted with stone axes, and possibly throwing spears. Females would have gathered food from vegetable sources and kept their children close to them to ensure their safety. The groups would also have taken care of those who were injured, elderly and sick. Humans of today were hunter-gatherers before the time of agricultural development and it is believed that H. Erectus were the first human beings to be living in this manner.

The belief is shared by a lot of paleoanthropologists H. was erectus had an adequate capacity to vocalize. The face that is flattened of H. Erectus indicates that teeth were not utilized for defense or attack. The flattened face offered H. Erectus with an enhanced capability to produce sophisticated vocal sounds. The neck vertebrae of H. the erectus look similar to modern humans and bigger than the hominins of earlier times and suggest that they could create complex sounds. While not able to speak like we use the term , or having a sophisticated spoken language H. Erectus may certainly have had the ability to communicate effectively with one another through distinct sounds.

With the help of their improved communications capabilities, elders may have taught others how to creating stone tools. Tool making of tools by H. erectus was very efficient. The Zhoukoudian cave in China in which remains of 45 Homo erectus people were discovered there was a ground covered with many stone-made tools. These tools were utilized by all members of the group. Analysis of the patterns of wear on surface of the tools suggests that the tools were designed generally used for cutting wood, slicing open animal carcasses as well as scraping bones and hides breaking bones, and digging out roots. While certain shapes were for specific tasks but wear analysis suggests they were mostly used according to the way the user needed currently. Certain of these tools feature a form that suggests they were made to be throwing disks, and it is speculated that they were used to hunt.

The time that H. erectus migrated out of Africa and into Europe, it is believed that they could create rafts from scratch and make more sophisticated watercraft. It is also believed they could have built their own tools from wood, like spears, containers, and bowels. Additionally, they could have constructed items made from hides, including backpacks and water sacks, to allow them to carry their possessions as well as water and food on their long journeys. They may also have made clothes from hides in order to keep warm in the colder temperatures of Asia. Unfortunately, wood and hides aren't well preserved for long periods of time and thus evidence that would help us understand more definitively what H. Erectus was living does not exist.

We have also found no evidence that suggests the level of sophistication in H. Erectus societies, with the only evidence of their existence being few fossilized bones, and stone tools. So it is here where we have to search for clues. In a few locations located in Africa there are forged blades that are far too massive to be used in a practical manner. It is believed that they may serve a ceremonial function for example, a way to show strength or to convey to prospective members the potential of a man as hunter with a lot of power. These rituals are an example of the expressions of the earlier times of culture.

H. Erectus are believed to have been found in caves, in which caves were found. This is proven by the discovery that have fossilized H. Erectus bones found in caves, along with the bones of animals they ate. The bones of animals show evidence of being cut and then smashed with stone tools, in contrast to having marks of predatory teeth on the bones. This suggests that the bones that were found in the cave weren't transported by bears or lions however, they were carried there by H. Erectus people. It is believed that H. Erectus might also have constructed simple huts with the help of materials including skins and timber but neither would be recorded in the archeological records.

Evidence of this type of construction of huts has been discovered in France in the region of France, where fascinating rings of stones that have been arranged in oval designs have been discovered during the time of H. Erectus's existence. It has been suggested they are the foundation of simple huts, in which the stones were used to support hides that were suspended above basic wooden constructions. This is a method that has been employed by humans of all ages to construct a basic tent. The design of the rocks suggest structures that can accommodate up to 40 persons in the approximate size of a family. Such interpretations are however heavily contested by other paleoanthropologists, who say that the stones could just represent a natural arrangement. We do not have any conclusive evidence that such structures were ever being built by H. the erectus. It is likely that they never will be, however it is not unreasonable to think of H. the erectus building simple huts in order to defend them from weather and other elements.

Being a great explorer H. erectus successfully populated most of the world and spread across Africa through what is today Europe and Europe, Middle East, India, China and Indonesia. This broad spectrum that was characterized by a wide range of environments and climates caused H. Erectus populations dispersing. The fossil record shows that localized physiological changes are evident to be observed among H. Erectus populations that lived across the broad spectrum of continents they lived on. The inevitable outcome was the development of different hominin species divergent from H. the erectus.

Chapter 7: The Spear Thrower - Homo Heidelbergensis

H. Erectus was spread throughout Africa in both Eurasia and was subject to environmental pressures, which pushed populations in particular to develop adaptive traits. As individuals moved between different regions they merged their gene pool and the traits that were most beneficial were retained. In this way, H. Erectus was able to evolve to become a stronger body and an intelligent brain. At times, the distinctive characteristics that were developed gave it advantages, and the localized populations could be able to evolve into an entirely new species. The new species will usually replace the original species. This is the way that new species typically appear for all animals. This is the way H. Habilis evolved from Australopithecus as well as H. the erectus came originated from H. Habilis.

This was the case for the species that would arise from, and eventually replace H. the erectus. Enter Homo heidelbergensis. H. Heidelbergensis was discovered about 800,000 years ago in Africa and rapidly expanded across the continent and also throughout Europe and eventually into Asia. It was displaced by H. Erectus when they expanded their territory, H. heidelbergensis drove the species that they evolved to extinction 450,000 years in the past. H. heidelbergensis themselves ultimately experienced the same fate and disappeared out of fossil records around 240,000 years long ago.

Named in honor of the German city of Heidelberg in the vicinity of where the first fossils belonging to the species were discovered, later discoveries have also been found across Ethiopia, Tanzania, Zambia, South Africa, Italy, France, England, Hungary, Greece and Spain. The fossils associated with H. heidelbergensis were very limited and sporadic. Therefore, for a long time, those reflected in our collection of the few fossils that we had were simply called "proto" Homo sapiens. They were not generally considered an individual species, but were thought to be a signifying some kind of gradual shift between H. Erectus with modern-day humans. Some paleoanthropologists questioned whether the findings were not indicative of any distinctive transition. They believed that the unusual fossils may simply be distinct subsets of H. Erectus that created their own distinctive adaptive traits.

In the 1990's, in the 1990's in the Sierra de Atapuerca region of northern Spain an abundance of human fossils were discovered in deep, dry caves. The caves contained both the bones of the people who lived there and various aspects of their daily lives. This still operating archeological excavation site yielded over 5500 fossils that represent approximately 32 people. Additionally, hundreds of animal and stone bones have been discovered within the human fossils. The oldest dates back to 350,000 years ago, the fossils comprise the entire cranium as well as fragments of other bones as well as a complete pelvis lower jaws and teeth foot, leg, arm and hand bones vertebrae and the ribs. More then 90% of the fossils that are that are attributed to H. heidelbergensis, these findings have convinced the paleoanthropology field that they are dealing with a unique species.

The Dominant of H. Heidelbergensis. The locations of major finds are identified by the Map.

Based on Spanish fossils H. Heidelbergensis had the brain size of 1250cm3, which was about half-way between H. Erectus and us. They were massive physically with males averaging 5'9 inches high (1.75 millimeters) and weighing 130 pounds (62 kg) and females who weighed five feet two" (1.57 meters) with 112 kg (51 kilograms). Based on the large footprints left by fossilized bones that correspond to the places where tendons were attached, H. Heidelbergensis were strong and muscular. The small amount of H. Heidelbergensis fossils discovered in Africa suggests that these individuals were a bit more slim than their European peers. This could be due to the local adaptations to climate in which a more slender body offers an increased surface area for the body, resulting in greater efficiency in cooling during the hot temperatures of Africa. Its compactness is a benefit in keeping body heat warm even in colder Europe.

H. Heidelbergensis retained the distinctive brow arching the ridges of H. the erectus along with their low-sloping foreheads and the absence of a defined chin. These features were however not as prominent in H. Heidelbergensis as they were in H. Erectus. H. Heidelbergensis, however, was beginning to display the shape of a rounder skull instead of the more elongated skull casings of H. Erectus. H. Heidelbergensis was also continuing in its quest to display a face that was ever slimmer with the wide nose of H. Erectus becoming a slightly more vertical. Jaws of H. Heidelbergensis was a bit larger than modern humans, however, it was less than the jaw of H. Erectus. They also had the round dental arc that is typical of modern human beings, possessing teeth that were no bigger than our ones.

Alongside their physiology, we have also gained insights into the technological and social capability for H. heidelbergensis. Dental wear, for instance, indicates that they were primarily right-handed. Their morphology in their outside and middle ears is similar to ours which suggests that they could distinguish sounds just like we do. This could suggest they had some kind of primitive speech, however this is just speculation. One of the most important aspects of the discoveries in Spain was the fact that a large portion of the skeletons that were found appeared to have been intentionally buried. This suggests an advanced society, with rituals related to the passing of people. Perhaps , bands of H. heidelbergensis had begun to incorporate into their society ways of coping with the loss that comes with the death of a member.

Skull from H. Heidelbergensis (left) with the Facial Reconstruction (right). Notice Comparatively smaller jaw and Rounded Skull in comparison to their predecessors.

Another incredible find, located on the German site of Schoningen was the discovery of eight well-preserved wood throwing spears, as well as stone spearheads. They were found to be dated to the year 400,000 and were clearly designed to hunt. The spears were found with other tools made of wood, which were fortunately preserved by the extremely dry conditions that prevailed within the cave. It is believed that H. Erectus made wooden tools, however the natural decomposition of this materials results in the tools not having been preserved. Thanks to the Schoningen discovery, however, we now have proof conclusive that H. Heidelbergensis wasn't just constructed wooden tools and weapons as well, but also was adept at hunting big game. This is proven by the countless preserved bones from large animals discovered during the spear found. This includes rhinoceros and bear, hippopotamus, horse and deer. Hunting for such big preys suggests that H. Heidelbergensis was an skilled and organized hunter for groups.

In addition to producing wooden spears as well as stone spear point, H. heidelbergensis produced stone axes that were bifacial. They were constructed with greater technological sophistication than the spears created from H. erectus. Other materials were employed to create tools along with wood and stone, like deer antler and bone. The main difference between the tools made by H. Erectus lies in the level of specificization. The variety in the form of the tools made by H. Erectus was quite restricted. In contrast, H. Heidelbergensis stones wood, antler, as well as bone instruments were more sophisticated in their design and were specifically designed to serve more diverse uses.

Another characteristic of H. Heidelbergensis confirmed by research is the final utilization of flames. In caves, and in conjunction with H. Heidelbergensis fossils, we can see the specific remains of hearths. They are so common that it is possible to say that H. Heidelbergensis was able to generate fire on demand. The control of fire is likely to have been vital to survive the harsh winters that swept across Northern Europe as well as Asia. Hearths have been found in caves, however it is likely that H. Heidelbergensis also constructed shelters even when caves weren't readily available. Made of materials such as hides and wood the fire hearth would be situated inside each dwelling. It is also thought at least for most northern venturing bands that some kind of clothing was constructed to keep warm.

As H. Heidelbergensis fossils have been found all over Africa, Europe and Asia There was some controversy regarding the place where the species first developed. H. Erectus appeared to be flourishing throughout Europe and Asia in the region where fossil finds have been found as recently to 450,000 years. So some have argued that H. Heidelbergensis may have developed within Asia. However, others noted that fossils that are of H. heidelbergensis are very uncommon in Asia. Others paleoanthropologists have suggested that it has an African origin, and others disagreed the idea that H. Erectus appears to have disappeared from Africa and there were no fossils found in the region dating back to 1.4 millennia ago. There is a suggestion that H. Heidelbergensis could have evolved within Europe due to the many fossils found in this region.

These questions are very difficult to answer through paleontology (study of fossils) and archaeology (study of stone tools and other structures) records on their own. DNA analysis, however, is in a position to clearly establish the lines of descent. DNA was taken from fossils found in Spain as well as through methods that will be examined in greater detail in the following chapter, the authors discovered it was proven that H. heidelbergensis in fact originated out of H. erectus in Africa. Then, they quickly spread across Africa as well as across Europe and, to lesser degree into Asia. The migrating bands could have caused displacement of the populations of H. Erectus they encountered, even though in Asia both species coexisted approximately 450,000 years in the past. At this time, H. is believed to have been destroyed by competition forces from H. Heidelbergensis, or simply fell victim to environmental pressures they weren't able to change to.

Its fate H. Heidelbergensis, however, was already on the verge of sealing. By the time 300,000 years passed an extended severe cold period had begun to take hold across the globe. Then Earth was to be an increasingly colder and dryer planet for the following 200 years. Glaciers in the north pushed further southward, while deserts to the south began to spread outward. Plains dwindled, and jungles were arid. The immense strain that this long phase of climate change put on us humans pushed us to the edge of death as we tried for a way to live. From this experience, many human species would emerge each with skills and abilities that were far superior to the capabilities of the hominins prior to.

Man of the North - the powerful Neanderthal

A massive global cooling event started in the 300,000 year ago, and would have significant consequences for the growth of the human race. Evolutionary pressures already had pushed hominins to a continuous pattern of becoming more intelligent and social, as well as bigger, stronger and more adept in the creation and use of tools. The succession of ice ages intermittently occurring was set to begin and would last for more than 200 years, would challenge us to the limits of what previously. From it would emerge an amazing hominin species.

Actually two species of hominins emerged. When cooling began to occur across the globe, the consequences were distinct in the southern climes of Africa and Asia than in the more northern latitudes. Thus, the human populations that lived in Europe as well as Asia were subject to different stress in terms of evolution from the ones who resided in Africa. The populations from the north of H. Heidelbergensis were expected to develop into one species, whereas the southerly populations would develop into another. This chapter traces the evolution of the first.

Everybody has heard of the powerful Neanderthal or, more accurately, Homo neanderthalensis. Strong, heavy set, the greatest hunter from the north. Where did Neanderthal originate from? What ever transpired to Neanderthals? We're actually in a position of being able to answer these questions today with great certainty. This is due to the lack of moisture of the areas where H. neanderthalensis existed preserved the remains of many of them in good condition. Certain bones from Neanderthal are sufficiently preserved so that the DNA could be extracted and analysed. With DNA analysis available and from now on, we can get a better understanding of how hominins evolved and how they were connected to one another.

A genetic analysis carried out from 2016 on H. heidelbergensis DNA recovered from caves found in Spain was discovered to be similar to DNA that was found in the later Neanderthal. Thus, Northern populations of H. Heidelbergensis has already begun to separate from the African population about 350,000 years ago. The genetic evidence indicates that Neanderthal along with the current human lineage diverged very early in the development of H. heidelbergensis, probably at least seven50,000 years prior. This is because of the different temperatures in Africa and Eurasia and the restricted gene flow between these two populations H. heidelbergensis began to diversify into two species earlier in its existence. Because of this, H. Heidelbergensis populations within Africa are often known as H. rhodesiensis to differentiate them from the population of northern diversification in the center.

Homo Neanderthalensis is believed to have started to evolve into distinct species around 450,000 years ago, separating from H. Heidelbergensis. Then, it briefly co-existed with them for a short period of time. Between 300,000 to the 240,000 year mark, during the initial stages of the cooling phase There is fossil gaps where evidence from the two species H. heidelbergensis and H. Neanderthalensis are extremely rare. Fossil gaps are frequent in periods of rapid evolutionary change when intense environmental pressures lead to population decline. Only those who have the genes that are suited to survive in the extreme conditions of the present are able to continue to have offspring that then carry the genes forward. This led to the development of a species that was well-suited to the harsh conditions of glaciation. It was a species that was more sophisticated and stronger than those that had come before it. Two40,000 years ago, Neanderthal skulls were resurfacing in the fossil record of Europe in Europe and Asia. H. Heidelbergensis in contrast was gone.

Neanderthals were highly set in comparison to H. Heidelbergensis, with the average weight of 171lbs (78 kilograms) in males, and the 146 pounds (66 kg) for females. This is comparable to the present world average of 150 pounds for males and 13 pounds of females. Neanderthal are believed to have been extremely strong when compared to their muscular forebearer H. Heidelbergensis. The legs and their arms were particularly built strong with their bones being extremely thick in comparison to our. For a pound, they were stronger than modern humans and it is said that the typical Neanderthal female could easily outdo an imposing modern man in an arm wrestling.

Sites where the Most Neanderthal Fossils were Found. Ice Sheets from The Last Glacial Maximum are Indicated by the Blue Projection over Europe.

They were , however, a bit smaller than H. Heidelbergensis, which was approximately 5'6" for males (166 cm) and 5'6" in females (152 cm). They had larger bodies and limbs that were shorter as compared to H. Heidelbergensis, too. The decrease in height, rise in stockiness, and compressing of the legs are adaptation strategies for surviving cold climates, which reduces surface area and thus better preserving body heat. The evolution of the human body has occurred through hundreds of thousands of years of living in northern regions the entire anatomy of their body was created specifically to endure extreme hardships and the harshness of a cold environment.

H. neanderthalensis had a large rib cage that was shaped like a barrel and lacked a distinct chin and had a broad nose with a sloping forehead and a distinct occipital bunion (a bulge that runs to the back of the skull) which is all akin with H. heidelbergensis. Their noses that were wide were an adaptation to breathe cold, dry air. They also had big eyes that had a greater portion of their brains involved in visual processing than contemporary human beings. It is thought that the focus on vision was in order to counteract the long, dark winters that can occur when one moves toward the north. A genetic study from 2007 indicated that some people may have hair with blonde or red hair as well as lighter skin tone, as well as other adaptations to living in a climate that had low levels of sunlight. H. neanderthalensis also had an extremely large brain. The average capacity of their brains was 1,600 cubic centimeters (98 cubic inches) for males, and 1,300 cubic centimeters (79 cubic inches) in females. This is actually slightly bigger than humans of today which is a reflection of their larger body size.

An interesting find is the finding of bones from two Neanderthal children that were found in France and dates up to 250,000 years old. Children aren't often seen in fossil records due to their more delicate bones that are more susceptible to being preserved. It was discovered that infants were nursed up to 2.5 years old as is the norm for modern human beings who live in nomadic community. This is in contrast to the nursing time of up to five years in bonobos and chimpanzees. The skulls were examined in depth and the teeth were cut cross-sectionally. The results revealed layers of enamel formed with every year, similar to the rings on the tree. The analysis of these layers showed changes in nutritional status and incidence of illness in children as the seasons change. It was discovered that harsh winters slowed the availability of food and caused a significant rise in illnesses. Incredibly, the Neanderthal children were discovered to have ridges on their fingers. These are typical of Chimpanzees, and they are utilized to aid babies when they clutch onto their mother's fur. Thus, Neanderthal could have been extremely hairy in comparison to us. This is especially likely when you consider the coldness of their surroundings.

A Comparative Study of Homo Erectus (left), Homo heidelbergensis (middle) and Homo neanderthalensis (right), using reconstructions based on fossil Skulls. It is important to note that it is evident that the Heavy Brow Ridge and Large Protruding Jaw Lessen in time The Flat Nose and the Small Cranium grow in size over the course of time. The Forehead is sloping in H. Erectus is maintained along the Evolutionary Path into H. Neanderthalensis. The distribution of hair and Skin Colors as assumed by the Artist, but with no hard evidence to support these.

Early Neanderthal developed tools using methods of Achaeulean Technology. The tools they used however became more sophisticated around 160,000 years ago and they created what's called the Mousterian technology complex. Mousterian tools were constructed primarily using flint and were the same type of tool making that modern humans also employed. This advanced tool-making technique continued to be utilized up until around 40 000 years in the past. With their arsenal of wood and stone weapons and their strength, the Neanderthals would be formidable hunter.

Neanderthal also had a good control over fire to heat and cooking. Based on fossilized animal bones discovered in Neanderthal cooking sites They hunted deer, red deer Ibex, wild boar straight tusked elephants rhinoceros, and even mammoths. Animals like rhinoceros and elephants were accessible to Neanderthal because they were more widespread before the human appearance as well as predatory animals like bears, lions, and the wolves. It is believed that it that it was modern humans who hunted these animals until local extincture, whether for food or to limit the presence of dangerous animals, thereby shoving them into smaller and less remote areas.

Certain vegetable matter has been found in the Neanderthals' diet through the examination of their teeth as well as fossilized feces. However, similar to the Inuit from Northern Canada when they were hunting There was generally no food sources for the Neanderthal. It was due to very little vegetation available in the tundra that was adjacent to glaciers. Their digestive systems developed to consume a protein-rich diet.

A Neanderthal Skeleton that is positioned to be holding a wooden Spear with a Hardened Point. A reconstruction of the person is suggested to the right. Neanderthal may have had more body hair than shown in the image.

While the majority of Neanderthal fossils have been discovered in Europe and therefore, this is the likely region in which the species developed but the area of H. Neanderthalensis is believed to have expanded to the east as time passed. Prior to 130,000 years ago, Neanderthal fossils discovered within Northern Europe are not common however, they became abundant after that point. This is due to the existence of an interglacial, which saw glaciers retreat and global temperatures increased and especially so in the northern regions, as is the case today with global warming. It was also 130,000 years since the eastward movement of the glaciers began.

Originating from a homeland on modern-day Spain, France and Italy and stretching from north to England in the west and even as wide as Romania Later, Neanderthal spread outwards throughout Turkey, Iran and across the southern part of Russia along with Kazakhstan. Out of the over 400 Neanderthal individuals whose fossils have been discovered only 70 were discovered in the southwest region of Asia and the rest were discovered in Europe. This indicates that Europe remains the Neanderthals' primary base, while the eastward expansions were merely excursions. But this could also be a reflection of the greater intensity of effort to locate hominin fossils Europe as opposed to Asia and we could someday revise our perception of this.

The amount of Neanderthal who traversed the Earth is believed to be a small number likely to be less than 150,000 people living at any point in time. The limit on the density of population was caused by the difficult environment and climate which they developed and lived. The extent and spread of Neanderthal sites as well as genetic evidence suggests that Neanderthals were smaller, less isolated groups than the human species further south. This is due to the dispersed nature and limited resources for food available.

The analysis of DNA extracted from Neanderthal bones shows that, within a particular Neanderthal group, males were of a common lineage whereas females did not. It is therefore believed that the groups were formed by close males and females. traded within groups. Also, it is believed because of the low genetic variation among people within groups, that some degree of interbreeding was likely to have occurred. When Neanderthal advanced to the east in the east, the thin and sparse population could have diminished interactions between groups, which would have reduced chances to exchange partners. Additionally, it could have diminished the amount of interaction between western and eastern population centers. In the course of time, populations of individuals are isolated within Russia and into Siberia started to develop in a different direction from Neanderthal.

Approximate Neanderthal Range Early Neanderthal Range Shown in Pink, Late Neanderthal Range in Blue. Notice that the Northern The Extent of Colored Areas is correlated with what is known as the Edge of the Glacial Sheets.

In 2008, in the Denisova Cave in Siberia a really unique discovery was discovered. The cave was the site of earlier Neanderthal fossils. Then an additional small collection of fossils were discovered they were believed to be part of H. neanderthalensis. The fossils are able to fit in the hand's palm comprised of just a finger bone as well as a toe bone, and two teeth. Finger bones were large and strong, indicating massive and strong hands, which is that are typical for Neanderthal. The fossils were dated at less than 100,000 years old, and the extreme dryness and cold of the area had allowed them to be preserved enough so that DNA could be extracted as well as other evidence of Neanderthal. However, when the DNA was analysed it was revealed to not be Neanderthal or modern humans. The DNA indicated a new species later dubbed Homo denisova.

The DNA was very similar to the DNA of Neanderthal and, without DNA analysis, no distinction due to fossil variation could have been detected. However, the paleoanthropology community concluded that the distinctions evident in the DNA evidence were enough to justify a new designation of species. The fossil that was identified as belonging to a 13-year-old girl who lived at around 90,000 years old, was found to have the genetics of a Neanderthal mother and an Denisovan father. Genetic tests revealed that Denisovan people had on average 17 percent Neanderthal genes. Therefore, the two groups were different but clearly capable of breeding. The Denisovan DNA is distinct as compared to Neanderthal which suggests that they were experiencing divergence because of the geographical isolation and climatic variations.

Neanderthal as well as Denisovan Migration from H. heidelbergensis.

H. Neanderthalensis and their close relatives H. denisova were able to excel at living in the cold landscapes beneath the mile-high glaciers in Europe as well as Asia. However, they would eventually be the victims of over-specialization. In order to be able to endure cold temperatures, they were forced to battle against the physiological disadvantages of their massive body weight. A bigger body requires more food to nourish it. It is believed that Neanderthal had to consume far more food than modern humans on a regular basis. The digestive system of Neanderthals likely was able to be able to digest meat efficiently, as is the case for leopard or wolf. However, ice-age periods do not remain forever, and the glaciers in which Neanderthal did well was about to come to an end.

After the ice had receded and the temperature began to rise the herds dispersed. the barren landscape of tundra was replaced by forest. Herds of large slow animals were replaced by swift deer and rabbits. It became difficult for Neanderthal to get the massive quantities of meat that they needed to eat. With the increasing temperature and the change in the environment an outsider entered the territory of Neanderthal. They were much larger that Neanderthal as well. Their presence along with the alteration of the environment, placed a tremendous stress on Neanderthal populations.

Within a short period, the populations of Neanderthal were destroyed. Their food sources of choice disappeared. The bipedal hominins that have entered their ancestral territory has made it difficult for them to hunt on areas. They were also forced to ever-more secluded areas. While certain Neanderthal may have been driven northwards however, many of them retreated westward due to invasions in the eastern direction. Based on fossil evidence , their most secluded strongholds appear to be in Spain in which they were forced to survive on the bare minimum of sources of sustenance in a forest environment that was not compatible with their ancestral lineage.

Findings from Spain during 2017 that showed Neanderthals that date to around the time of their demise suggested they ate meatless diets.

They lived on pine nuts, moss and mushrooms. It's like an lion being forced to live on vegetables and fruits. The desperateness of their circumstance is evident. Bones from 12 Neanderthals found in northern Spain dating back to the time of 50,000 years be evidence that the victims were killed and defleshed. This indicates that dire circumstances led to others turning to commit cannibalism. Similar findings from other areas and different time intervals suggest that Neanderthal could have actually frequently turned to cannibalism to get through difficult times.

A Hypothetical Imaginary of A Hypothetical Scenario of Neanderthal Elder who is a young. Although they possess unique facial characteristics, their resemblance with Modern Humans is Evident. It is suggested that If you put a suit and tie on an Neanderthal and gave him A Shave, You'd be able to walk him down the Modern Street and not raise More than a few heads. The individuals depicted above are shown as being rather pale Skinned. Genes that favor light Skin have been discovered within Neanderthal DNA. Neanderthal might have been significantly hairier than the grown Man The evidence suggests.

The Neanderthal were forced to extremes and eventually disappearance by this new threat to their land, and were compelled to leave Africa and discover the world through the spread of warmth. Bipedal walker, with many similarities to Neanderthal but this rival had a more sharp mind and was more organized in their communities, was able to speak clearly defined words using their mouths and, perhaps most importantly, they swarmed over their land in huge quantities. At a time of 25,000 years, the massive Neanderthal giants, who dominated the north, disappeared from fossil records forever.

Chapter 8: Our Emergence - Homo Sapiens

The invaders who had encroached on the ancestral homelands of Neanderthal are known under their scientific title Homo sapiens. Homo sapiens was the scientific name assigned to Carl Linnaeus in 1758 to the hominin species that was unique to. The word 'homo' is Latin meaning 'man' and 'sapiens' is a reference to "wise". While Neanderthal was busy developing from H. Heidelbergensis, which was found within the northerly regions of Eurasia, H. sapiens was also busy transforming from H. Heidelbergensis located on the African continent. Being able to evolve in warmer temperatures than those found throughout Asia and Europe the new 'smart species rapidly expanded all over the Eurasian continents after glaciers receding. You've probably already guessed, the new hominin species was us - modern human.

It is believed that we evolved as a distinct species around 300,000 years ago. However, the exact date is difficult to determine due to the fossil gap that existed between two million and 260,000 years in the past. This corresponds to a time of evolutionary change and the low density of hominins across the globe. At the time those same forces that led to glaciers in the north resulted in a reduction in temperatures on Southern continents. While the temperature was still moderate, the climate was becoming extremely dry. The result was that a lot of the landscape changed to desert and dry savannah. The harsh conditions forced us to develop further in order to survive.

Two theories exist on how humans have evolved into modern-day humans. Human evolution as a species could be a local phenomenon where a tiny isolated group of people in Africa evolved through genetic mutation and all the adaptations needed for the transformation into human. They would have dispersed and forced out other within

Africa. This was the old knowledge, but today this theory is regarded as incomplete. Another possibility is that the different groups comprised of H. heidelbergensis throughout Africa each has distinctive advantages to evolution due to an uncontrolled genetic change. After admixture, the various groups, and as the mates of communities exchanged and the most advantageous genes between them were shared and, in most cases, conserved. The result was an entirely new species that gathered all the top genetic adaptations useful to survive in harsh conditions.

The limited fossil discoveries from this time of evolutionary change suggest this more ambiguous model of evolution to be the reality. The fossils exhibit a wide range of contemporary and archaic characteristics. Humans that evolved at the age of 300,000 years ago could have displayed an extremely wide range of traits and individuals from certain communities displaying physical characteristics distinct from those of other communities. These early members from our species have been commonly called 'archaic' human beings.

Between 300,000 to the year 200,000 These physiological variations among us were masked and smoothed through continual admixture until we became an increasingly physiologically consistent species. The anatomically modern humans are often known as"Anatomically Modern Humans'. Also, they are referred to as'modern humans. The first fossil found that has been classified as belonging to modern humans were the Omo remains'. They were discovered between 1967 and 1975 through Richard Leakey and his research team in the Omo National park of Ethiopia The fossils were dated to around 195,000 year old. The discovery included two incomplete skulls and jaws as well as four, and an ankle bone and a variety of teeth and other bones that were fragmented. The fossils were described as with some archaic features to the bones.

Another important discovery of AMH was found in 1997 in Herto located in the northern part of Ethiopia. Also known as 'Herto Man', the discovery comprised of three well-preserved skulls that were dated between 160,000 and 160,000 years. The skulls had some primitive features, which are common in the early stages of AMH. One skull was a child's and another belonged to a male who was young and another to a mature male. The male who was grown was able to hold a total cranium volume of 1450 cubic centimeters (88 cubic inches) that was within the human norm of modern times. The skulls was well-rounded instead of being elongated. The paleoanthropologists who came across the fossils believed the fossils as belonging to a sub-species of humans, and named them Homo sapiens Idaltu. However, the range of human physiologies in early humans is extensive, so these fossils should really be described as Homo sapiens.

Modern humans have a distinct skull shape that is different from the other hominins. Our skull is rounded with a high forehead required to accommodate our massive forebrain. All early humans had an elongated skull , with strong downward inclined foreheads. Thus, where our forebrains rest above the eyes of ours, those was positioned in front of their eyes. We also have a shorter eyebrow ridge, as well as a distinctive chinthat is reflecting our shrinking dentary. Humans from earlier times had bigger jaws and the brow ridge protruding outwards that crossed both eyes. Also, they had an distinctive "occipital bun," or bulge at the sides the skulls. This feature was used to anchor massive neck muscles to muscles we could not keep.

Comparative Study of the Form and Relative size of Hominin Skulls. Neanderthal can be seen as being larger than our own species, indicating their larger overall body size. The jaw of Neanderthal protrudes less than H.

Erectus, Despite it is the Large Brow Ridge and Elongated Skull are preserved.

Our skulls are also a reflection of the continuing trend towards relatively less sized jaws, teeth and jaws for hominins. We generally have lower and smaller faces as well as more flexible and slim jaws than the hominins we share a relationship with. The constant use of fire for cooking of food diminished our dependence on strong jaws, big neck muscles, large teeth, and protruding dentition. When the need for a strong jaw diminished, our jawline decreased in size and drew back. The use of these features also helped to improve our vocal capabilities, allowing us to make more precise and wide variety of sounds.

In terms of our height, we were similar to Neanderthals. H. Heidelbergensis as well as H. Erectus, with 175-165 centimeters (5 five feet, 5 inches to 5 feet 9, inches) in males , and between 152 and 165 cm (5 feet to 5 feet) for females. Humans of today are much less robust species than other hominins with taller statures, particularly when compared with our northern counterpart Neanderthal. Our leanness is due to our African ancestral roots and the need to shed body heat. However, we have a lower muscle mass, and density have also decreased. In comparison the H. erectus, H. Heidelbergensis as well as H. neanderthalensis, we are weaklings.

The reduction in muscle mass came about due to our ability to manufacture and use advanced equipment. We no longer required huge muscles. Massive muscles consume lots of calories, even when they are not being used. A body that consumes less calories is more able to be fed and is more likely to endure times of hunger. So early modern humans with smaller muscles are more likely endure and reproduce. Therefore, as time goes on, we are more fragile. We relied less on the body's strength to survive, as we had mastered the power of a higher mind.

Mammals that weigh around our size have a brain that has about 200 cubic centimeters in size. Our brain is, approximately 1400 cubic centimeters. While it's only 2 or three percent from our weight our brains consume 25 percent of our energy at the rest of our bodies. This is in contrast to 8percent for the great Apes. Due to our increasing dependence on our brain's calorie-hungry capabilities our muscles are inevitably weakened in order to stop our calorie needs from soaring. In this extremely harsh and violent world where all life fights to survive, relying on canines, claws and muscles isn't usually considered a viable strategy for survival. However, we were able to use it.

We did more than just get it done however, we also excelled. We were close to extinction and enhanced our survival capabilities by enhancing the capabilities of the sole resource available to count on. Then, this new intelligence pushed us from Africa and then back to the global stage. But this time , there was no retreat. We were staying. We would soon prove to be the supreme form of animal that exists on earth.

www.ingramcontent.com/pod-product-compliance
Lightning Source LLC
Chambersburg PA
CBHW050407120526
44590CB00015B/1858